LIFE'S METAMORPHOSIS OF THE SOUL

Edward L. Dean, Ph.D.

Diligence Publishing Company
Bloomfield, New Jersey

Scripture references are from the King James Version and the New International Version of the Bible.

LIFE'S METAMORPHOSIS OF THE SOUL

Copyright © 2021 Edward L. Dean, Ph.D.
c/o Diligence Publishing Company
P.O. Box 2476
Bloomfield, New Jersey

All Rights Reserved

No part of this book may be reproduced in any form without the written permission from the publisher except for brief passages included in a review.

To contact Dr. Dean to preach or speak at your church, organization, seminar, or conference email: contact@dpc-books.com

LIFE'S METAMORPHOSIS OF THE SOUL

ISBN: 978-1-7331353-9-9

Printed in the United States

TABLE OF CONTENTS

DEDICATION 5
INTRODUCTION 7
1. The Early Years: 1941 to 1953 Experiences 11
2. The Time of Transition 17
3. The School Years – Time of Dispensation 21
4. A Turning Point in Life's Journey 27
5. The Time for Departure 31
6. The Unexpected Frontier 35
7. Personal Growth and Cultural Challenges 37
8. Destiny Phase Activation 41
9. New Business and Personal Growth Activation .. 47
10. Confronting Ego and Pride 51
11. Destiny's Calling 55
12. The Coming Journey 61
13. Life's Unexpected Divergence 67
14. A Season of Validation 71
15. The Unexpected Request 77
16. The Past and Post Season Beginning 83
17. The Beginning of the Latter Days of Life 87
18. The Signs of Change 91
19. Promotion and Organization Transition 95
20. HAC'S Unexpected Leadership Transition 99
21. Moving Into a Part of Your Destiny 103
22. Come Business and Unrelated Activity 107
23. A Stirring Up of the Eagle's Nest 111

24. Business Expansion and Gateway into the Unforeseen 115
25. Strategy of the Forward Engineering Presence 119
26. A Strengthening of My Christian Faith 123
27. Moving Toward Change 125
28. International Ministry Transition 129
29. An Unexpected Inquiry 133
30. Prayer Is My Direction Finder 137
31. Changes That Come with Time 141
32. Moving Forward Without Conditions 145
33. The Unexpected Request 149
34. Discovering My Spiritual Strengths and Weaknesses 153
35. Extended Omnibus Responsibilities 157
36. A Time of Challenges to the Soul 163
37. A Trying of Your Faith 167
38. When My Income Began to Change 171
39. God Watches Over His Word to Perform It 177
40. Believe and Worship God: Appreciate the Blessings 181
41. Life's Unexpected Effects and Faith 185
42. God Is the Author and the Finisher of My Faith 189
ABOUT THE AUTHOR 193
ORDER INFORMATION 195

DEDICATION

I dedicate this book to my biological family, especially to my wife, Rose, my constant encourager, and to my spiritual family whose consistent love and fellowship served as an inspiration to share my life metamorphosis that may be a challenge to many to introspectively review their life's journey. My biological sisters, Claudette (Tet) and Thelma Jean (TJ), and her daughter Tammie, my niece, brought me to salvation after a mid-week service in Los Angeles. They're very strong believers and on this stormy raining night, I believe they were led by the Holy Spirit to bring me, I was like a lamb, to Tammie's home for the conversion. Surprisingly, with tears flowing, I heard myself say, "I fear failure."

They each in their own way over all the years have answered any doctrinal and/or spiritual questions I had. My tenacious sister TJ was my constant reminder that I was called by God, and not necessarily to a pulpit, and she always told me to stop trying to ignore her. Her loving support has only become stronger throughout the years.

Then came the unexpected blessing of blessings, I believe sent by the Holy Spirit, a couple and two families with their children wanting to have breakfast together after church services. These gatherings began to grow, with a few other young spiritual brothers and sisters, (now sons and daughters) with their children into what felt like our family's fellowship. My wife and I had no family in New Jersey, and for the first time, the Holy Spirit said to us, not audibly, *"These are the children of your maturity."*

Truly their love and support to my wife and I have consistently gone beyond what one could think or imagine.

INTRODUCTION

On Friday evening, April 19, 2019, my church was in celebration of the Christian "Good Friday" which also happens to be the same day of the "Jewish Passover." The pastor had invited a guest Messianic Christian pastor to teach on the Jewish Passover and the meaning of all the associated utensils in conjunction to Jesus' teachings at the "Last Supper." The teaching was outstanding and inspiring.

I suddenly found myself thinking of the many spiritual and supernatural experiences I have had since my very early childhood starting at approximately five years of age. I felt compelled to begin memorializing those experiences that eventually brought necessary changes to my soulish life. My soulish life is really inclusive of my entire life's journey, which will expose good and not so good life experiences that will eventually change and impact your soul.

Needless to say, I had no understanding of what it meant to have your soul impacted. After many years, I came to understand that your soul is your mind, will, emotions, intellect, and your imagination. Every human has a temperament which is housed within your soul and is structured into the following three areas which will reflect your natural behavioral tendencies and your learned behavior in how you deal with life issues.

Inclusion is the socialization, associations, surface relationships and general intellectual exchange made when interacting with others in different worldly places/locations of people.

Control is the area that reflects your decision-making capability.

Affection is those very special and close relationships. Your soul, along with your body and spirit, defines the totality of every individual. An impacting change in the body, soul or spirit can have a domino effect in the other areas (i.e. good or bad).

The world's order of the greater influence to the soul of mankind is their priority order of the

INTRODUCTION

body, soul, and spirit. The body can and does promote inappropriate behavior, both physical and mental to the soul. Whereas mankind's spiritual objective is to reverse world's order priority to spirit, soul, and body. The beginning of the transformation of the soul will begin to negate the soul's improper behavior and decisions influenced previously by the body. The subtle changes to the soul are indicative of the metamorphosis taking place in your life's attitude and behavior.

I write on this subject matter to hopefully stimulate thought-provoking desires to seek an understanding of the true reality of the unseen spiritual realm, which is eternal, at times releasing spiritual and godly power that comes through it.

Supernatural events and circumstances occur/manifest in countless ways and each is unique to the individual, and/or a people (e.g. Israel's exodus from Egypt).

From the genesis of my first spiritual encounter as a very young child, the intended purpose of being transparent is apparent in describing the experience. It's important that you understand how the Holy Spirit deals with you in a supernatural way, and it may or may not be as described in this book. How the Holy Spirit deals with you is unique, personal and is associated with the purpose for which you're called.

In this book, I am still seeking understanding for having been chosen by the Holy Spirit for a purpose beyond my understanding. That being said, I began to see a transformation of supernatural and subtle experiences manifest in my life. With that in mind, I suspect you also can be expected to encounter spiritual and supernatural experiences over the course of your life. That being the case, as you read this book, look for signs or the beginning of signs of metamorphosing/change like the transformation of the cocoon to the butterfly. Ask yourself what stage of your soul's metamorphosis are you in today (i.e. Reflection and Meditating). I have added a section called Reflection and Meditating at the end of each chapter for you to use to help identify what stage you are in pertaining to your own personal soul's metamorphosis.

CHAPTER 1

The Early Years: 1941 to 1953 Experiences

As the unction to engage in writing on this book's subject matter came to me, my immediate thought went to my first encounter of what I believe was a spiritual experience as a child of approximately five years of age. My persistent recollection over the years has been my remembrance of riding in the rear seat of my parents' automobile. I believe we were coming from a drive-in theater. As we continued down the darkened highway, there was a fair for whites only near the highway. This was the decade of the 1940s in Jackson, Mississippi.

I was so intrigued seeing the Ferris wheel from our car, I thought Santa Claus was waving at me from the top of the Ferris wheel, and I thought to myself, *"I wish Santa Claus and Jesus were my relatives."*

As I thought of this experience many years later, the Santa Claus wish as a young child of approximately five years of age was obvious. On the other hand, the desire for Jesus to be my relative had to have come out of a deep desire of my heart, and I believe, encouraged by the Holy Spirit.

I was the first born of my parents and also the first-born grandchild of my mother's parents, who had ten children. My father was the youngest child of his parents who had seven children. Many families of the previous generations/cultures leading up to the 1950s have had a strong love bond for their children, but they usually were outwardly not expressed or demonstrative. Yet, all in the community were aware of the family's closeness. The African Americans knew the importance of being close as a family unit. To some degree interoperating as a village was to look out for one another. Even though this was the 20th century, the white southern racists still thought and behaved like their predecessors.

As a child of color, you're taught where you can go and not go. This leads me to share the following encounter which was indicative of the white southern racist attitude regarding an active desire to take the life of a young Black boy. However, this planned intention was blocked by a supernatural action as follows: It was a fall season and I was raking leaves with my mother when a white man drove up in a black car and began to blow his horn. I thought it was the postman. My mother said, "Don't go out there."

I can only assume that my mother went somewhere temporarily because I found myself by the man's driver side front car door. Suddenly, he lifted up a dagger! Fear griped me and I froze in place. Just as suddenly, the man put the dagger down and said, "Your mother called you," and rapidly sped off.

I don't know what he saw or heard but my mother was not in the yard area, nor did she even mention the white man that I thought was the postman. This was not how my mother, who was extremely protective, would have acted, especially when she had told me not to go out where the white man was. I believe the white man heard and/or saw something that apparently frightened him. It seems this experience was erased from my mother's mind.

We lived in a quasi-rural area of Hinds County, in the capital and State of Jackson, Mississippi in the 1940s; it still had 19th Century remnants of living conditions, farming, poor infrastructure and an unchanged segregationist mentality. There were areas/locations that young children were forbidden to go, such as the Pearl River, without an adult or mature teenager. This river was known to have had alligators, water moccasin snakes, large turtles, etc.

Being a typical adventuresome young boy, I slipped off and went to the river without an escort. The river appeared muddy but what was extraordinarily unusual was, on the bank above the river was gushing spring water, extremely cold and very clean looking. I felt very compelled to stoop and drink. The water was not only very cold but sweet to the taste. I managed to get home without anyone knowing where I had been.

In the year 2000 I went to the nation of Israel and the experience of finding and drinking the cold spring water from the riverbank as a young child came back to my memory with meaning.

Even though we moved into more of an urban area, called Georgetown, many families took with them a rural culture and lifestyle suitable for establishing a vegetable garden and or for raising a variety of chickens and other fowls to cut the cost of living expenses. As it turned out, my father's godmother raised chickens in her backyard. At times I would leave her home through her backdoor to go home. On this particular day as I proceeded to walk through her backyard, a rooster I did not see jumped on my back. I was shocked because I did not go inside the fenced in area where all the chickens were kept.

Needless to say, a lifelong phobia of any type of fowls was the end result of the rooster attack. As I ponder about this experience, I never saw the rooster coming or when he left my shoulders. That being said, the rooster became my father's godmother's main dinner course.

Reflection and Meditating

_____
_____
_____
_____

LIFE'S METAMORPHOSIS OF THE SOUL

CHAPTER 2

The Time of Transition

When I was 12 years old, my mother's brother was honorably discharged from the United States Army at the end of the Korean conflict. Upon his returning home to Jackson, Mississippi, a decision was made between him and my mother to move to Los Angeles, California, where some of their other brothers and sisters had moved at the closing of school for the summer.

My uncle, mother, two sisters, one brother and a first cousin my age were packed into my uncle's automobile and left for Los Angeles, California in June of 1953. Three days later, early in the morning we arrived in Los Angeles to my mother's sister's home.

I took a walk in the neighborhood and was extremely surprised when a young white boy, approximately my age, spoke to me in a very kind and friendly way. I was so surprised that I told my mother.

"Boy," I thought, *"this is certainly not Jackson, Mississippi."*

This was truly a new beginning that brought with it a new culture.

It was amazing that I had not given thought about the two years prior to this time when my father and mother made arrangements and placed my younger sister and I on a train sending us to Los Angeles to spend the summer with my father's sister. Even more amazing was my being shocked when my mother kissed me when we were being placed on the train. It was a time of being exposed for the first time to an environment of integration, seeing a television for the first time, including seeing the Pacific Ocean. This was a summer of attending an integrated grammar school, competing in a variety of games, and going to the beach with all its rides and games in Long Beach, California.

The inevitable ending of summer brought an unexpected surprise in my having to attend a public school for the first time. We had attended a private school, Grace Lutheran Christian Day School, which I attended through the fifth grade. Sharing my summer experiences was delightful as in describing television which no one had ever seen or known about. I spoke of watching a movie that was a part of the TV's programs, and I described it as a picture show within a picture show. We all knew about movie theaters or picture shows.

My sixth-grade year in attending the public school of Mary C. Jones Grammar School brought changes in how we attended school. For instance, walking to school and not being driven by family and/or some designated individual. Our moving into the quasi suburban area of Georgetown allowed us to meet children that attended the same grammar school we attended, and they befriended us. It was a safe area, and it appeared a substantial number of people knew someone that knew your family.

This sixth-grade year in a sense brought an end to a village-like atmosphere but replaced it with an expansion of knowing more children without necessarily knowing their parents. There was no more religious teaching or religious special programs that parents attended to watch their children participate in various roles. As I give thought to these annual events, I realize it was a form of training for public speaking. It was foundation setting for the soon coming junior high school years.

Reflection and Meditating

CHAPTER 3

The School Years – Time of Dispensation

We stayed with my mother's sister the first year of our moving to Los Angeles, and I was registered in the seventh grade at Bret Hart Junior High School. The junior high school years were the seventh grade through the ninth grade. I attended two junior high schools (Bret Hart and Gompers) before graduating to Fremont High School.

The class attending culture was quite an experience, coming from a history of all subjects taught from a single classroom by the same teacher to a homeroom to begin each day and attending seven separate classes with corresponding teachers.

The junior high school I attended was apparently well budgeted. Primarily because it was located in an upper white middle class income area. This junior high school had what others did not have. It had required swimming lessons for all students, after school organized sports in coordination with local park management, art classes, miscellaneous music lessons, vocal and/or instrument classes, etc.

The classes were all very demanding, such as my seventh grade English class required the reading of the novel *"Les Misérables"* and the writing of a book report.

This junior high school was a tremendous blessing in that I was exposed to and became a proficient athlete in the sports in which I was a participant. I participated in basketball, football, softball, handball, and some elements of gymnastics. The great majority of my time during the summer in particular was spent at the park playing on the various teams.

Our first year in Los Angeles was great in that we all made the necessary adjustments in quickly embracing the west coast culture. Our family was finally able to move into our own home, and in doing so we had to transfer into a new school district.

The contrast between the two junior high school programs and class requirements was miles apart. In our second year, we all came to know a diversity of new friends as we did in the previous schools we attended.

The teachers and the quality of the teaching was pretty much the same as the other junior high school. However, the educational standards and programs were not in equal quality to the other school.

Moving into the outer edge of East Los Angeles (L. A.) was a noticeable shifting population move of some Caucasians to other areas of West L. A. and the San Fernando Valley areas. Unlike the south where segregation was legal and very overt, California was very subtle but effective when it came to segregation. We lived in the area for a year and moved back into a location where my mother's sister lived.

Our move, as it turned out, was back into the school district we began in. I was happy to transfer back into Bret Hart Junior High School where my journey began. Going into the ninth grade I tried to get an after-school job but was never successful. The ninth-grade year was one of both physical and mental growth that influenced how I dealt with different situations. One experience of particular interest was in dealing with a parakeet bird. That understanding would not come until late into my adult years. My brother, five years younger than I, bought and caged the parakeet he named Tommy. Tommy was extraordinarily wild and not touchable. Needless to say, my having a phobia of fowls, I had no desire or intention of going near the cage or touching the parakeet.

One night I was up late doing homework, and everyone was in bed when suddenly, I felt the parakeet light on my shoulder. I almost struck Tommy with my book, but he remained perched on my shoulder unafraid. I thought, *"I could like this bird."*

I held my finger out and he perched on it. I went back to the cage with Tommy perched on my finger, opened the cage door and he jumped in and perched on the swing in the cage.

I was amazed at the sudden tameness of the parakeet and how he got out of the cage with the door closed. I was so pleased with the experience when I went to bed. I was so anxious looking forward to seeing Tommy when I got up. I went into total shock to find Tommy on the bottom of his cage dead.

I didn't know what to think. I just accepted Tommy's (the parakeet's) death as a normal phenomenon, but something I would never forget.

Reflection and Meditating

LIFE'S METAMORPHOSIS OF THE SOUL

CHAPTER 4

A Turning Point in Life's Journey

Entering Fremont High School was truly a turning point in my life. I finally got a weekend job at a car wash where I worked throughout my three years in high school. My aunt (my father's sister) cosigned for me to have a clothing account in a men's store. It was a time of establishing new friendships and becoming legally responsible for acquired debt.

Based on my junior high school transcript grades, I was automatically placed in academic science courses which were college preparatory classes. I tried out for the junior varsity basketball team and became a first-string guard.

These high school years were times of growth in my study discipline, and growth in maturity as I became a young adult. I was a typical teenager, with a mirage of dreams and expectations.

I never had a girlfriend over this three-year period of time, but I had numerous female friends. This period of time was one of exploratory opportunities to pursue adventure in other areas only heard about, such as college fraternity houses to meet and socialize with known and new friends. Having a best friend with an automobile made a new venture possible.

Being a competitive high school athletic basketball player and gymnast, my knowledge of the geography of the various areas began to expand. This time of my life was an expansion awareness of cultures and recognition of other cultures, beliefs, and behaviors as it pertains to other ethnic groups.

In retrospect of a historical view at the integration of some schools and the competitiveness of athletes in sports, some still reflected a segregates' mentality. Once an event was over, like-racial groups socialized together. Even though the challenges were very proactive and great for integration, there was still a subtle mentality of prejudicial behavior.

That being said, overall, there was an atmosphere of acceptance throughout Southern California. There was a feeling of acceptance wherever you went, which was nothing like the south, especially Jackson, Mississippi. I had a proactive attitude of taking on challenges and did not fear rejection in the different environments.

My preparation for high school graduation was one of transitioning from an environment of control to one of self-control and discipline. It was during this period of graduation preparation that I would meet my first wife-to-be. Ironically, we never knew each other over our three years of attending the same high school.

Reflection and Meditating

LIFE'S METAMORPHOSIS OF THE SOUL

CHAPTER 5

The Time for Departure

My graduating from high school was the beginning of unknown milestones yet to come. My mother was the primary provider for our family, myself, two younger sisters and a younger brother, making it possible for me to begin becoming independent. My uncle's wife made it possible for me to get a job at a 5 and 10 cent department store, S & H Kress, right after graduation. My uncle soon thereafter cosigned for me to buy my first car. A close friend of my uncle and my mother rented a cottage court from my grandmother and allowed me to move in with him. This was another milestone that blessed me to be on my own and to register in a community junior college, Trade Tech Community College.

Truly I was blessed with love and favor leaving home at 18 years of age, with a bare minimum of expense obligations. I quickly mastered my job requirements and functions. I acquired an understanding of the California State College requirements as I registered for classes. As of September 1959, I began taking evening courses. I attended college for approximately twelve years before receiving a Bachelor of Science Degree.

Trade Tech Community Junior College was on the quarter system which was really beneficial in allowing more classes to be taken in less time as opposed to the semester system. As it turned out, I had the same professor for several business courses who worked at a corporation during the day. I mention this professor, Mrs. Douglas, because she became the key to my future entry into corporate positions.

I received A's in the courses I had taken with her, and she asked me would I go to take an exam at a corporation called Metropolitan. I took the exam and she told me I had done very well but I was Black, and the area of their need was in computers. Such was the continuous status quo beliefs and attitude of the 1960s, 1970s, et cetera with an unknown end to realize true equality. The basis of this corporation's rejection seems to have incentivized this professor to get me employment in a corporation where I would have an opportunity to exploit my potential. Within a two-week period from the point of rejection Mrs. Douglas asked would I go to downtown Los Angeles and take an exam from an employment placement agency owner, Mrs. Hawkins. Mrs. Hawkins reviewed the exam upon completion and stated she would contact me within two weeks.

As promised, Mrs. Hawkins did contact me within a two-week window at my place of employment. She offered me a position at an Aerospace Firm called Autonetics. Autonetics was a division of North American Aviation, also the owner of the Space Division, the architect and developer of the Apollo Command Module.

The position offered was one of service and support of technical writers.

I gave my southern boss a two-weeks' notice before leaving my position. He made me a financial offer not to leave, to no avail. We had discussions regarding my reasons for leaving. The Civil Rights movement had begun, and the demonstrators were picketing in front of the store. Our discussion ended with his comment that I was different from those out front, of which I disagreed and addressed my reasons. He gave me a bonus at the time of my leaving.

Reflection and Meditating

CHAPTER 6

The Unexpected Frontier

October 31, 1960, was the time which ushered into my life an unexpected, unheard of business known as the aerospace Industry. Needless to say, this job was the beginning of building a career path. This new position made training but also being proactive an absolute necessity in supporting technical writers. I decided to check into a high school to review drafting techniques and how to read blueprints. Only two to three weeks in evening classes was necessary to understand blueprint reading and drafting techniques.

A function of this job was the establishment and management of a blueprint station, which included the storage of technical manuals. By the end of my first year, I had an understanding regarding the technical manuals principles by providing service support to technical writers and draftsmen. This was a technical culture but also one of a social nature that extended from playing pinochle at work to some in their preferential whites-only communities.

During my second year, after many requests, I was given an opportunity to write and was successful in having the manual approved and certified by the military customer. After successfully writing the next two manuals, I was given a technical writer classification.

A salary increase came with the promotion to the technical writer classification. The promotion and salary increase were certainly an encouragement to continue my evening college courses. I also became engaged to my high school girlfriend.

Reflection and Meditating

_____
_____
_____
_____
_____
_____
_____
_____
_____
_____

CHAPTER 7

Personal Growth and Cultural Challenges

The advances made in business contributed to the increase in the prosperity in my relationship with my girlfriend. As our relationship flourished, more of an interaction with her parents occurred. Her mother and stepfather were not highly educated, but they were financially established as upper middle class. The stepfather was a paint contractor with employees, a property owner of numerous rental properties, and a man of ambitions.

I came to believe the cultural mentality and a belief of the family wasn't exactly compatible with and the same as mine. I found their friends and associates had similar values and cultural behavior which would eventually have an impact on my relationship with their daughter.

As our relationship eventually became more intimate, we got engaged. Our engagement was reluctantly accepted by her parents. At this time, in their minds, I believe there was a distinct difference in class and culture. This type of thinking and belief was a part of their generation. The stepfather's interaction with my mother really didn't go well for him, and very little interaction in the future took place. Needless to say, I didn't find much favor with the mother who had a personality of manipulation and control.

An unforeseen fracture and unexpected incident came in our relationship one night after I dropped off my fiancé after a date. I was driving home when suddenly a very intensive thought came to my mind saying to go back to her home. I went to her bedroom window, and I overheard her conversation of infidelity. Needless to say, this temporarily ended our engagement and set in motion two decades of challenges but opportunities to work through the issues and problems, my relentless bitterness, and my unforgiving attitude and resentment, to only find peace of mind and growth only comes through forgiveness, which comes through spiritual maturity.

An experience of this nature begins to reveal a true type of character demands that a person possesses and the struggle of pride that causes one to internalize and not communicate with anyone because of the pain and shame felt. This attitude and behavior demand resulted in absolute privacy that led me to a bout of three bleeding stomach ulcers that ended up requiring hospitalization.

The decade of the 1960's was strongly influenced by emotionally undulating negative and positive times that prevented consistent times of peace and happiness. This time of my life I would in the future reflect on because of the following thought that was completely illogical at the time, *"I ought to move to New Jersey"* and the T.V. news program that subsequently came on addressing rains and flood conditions in certain areas of New Jersey.

At the time I knew no one in New Jersey and never had a desire to move there. The thought didn't make sense, and I never gave it another thought for more than two decades.

The 1960s era was also a personal time of growth and an unexpected temporary setback in my aerospace industry career path. I received my first degree (an Associate of Arts Degree), purchased my first home in Los Angeles Morningside Park area and became a father of three children – two boys and a girl.

Reflection and Meditating

_____
_____
_____
_____
_____
_____
_____
_____
_____
_____
_____
_____
_____
_____
_____
_____
_____

CHAPTER 8

Destiny Phase Activation

In my fourth year at Autonetics, a division of North American Aviation, the technical writers' contract budget was reduced, and I was put on loan in the Department of Payroll and Timekeeping. My reputation as an excellent worker made constant overtime possible, which negated a loss of take-home income. Within two months, I was contacted by someone from Space Division, a division of North American Aviation, and the Apollo Program Office. I never discovered who recommended me for the open job position. Upon requesting permission from my technical writer manager, he informed several technical writers of the open position I was going to interview for. Nevertheless, I was interviewed and was offered the position, which I accepted and was transferred to the Apollo Program.

Transferring into the Apollo Program was extraordinarily exciting, but I soon came to realize the effects and impact of stressfulness. It occurred almost on a monthly basis, when an engineer would be taken out on a gurney. One of the stress factors was refining the Apollo Command Module design. Another was the contractual schedule for meeting aggressive milestone phases.

The department I was transferred into was the Apollo Configuration Management Office, an engineering support organization whose primary function was to ensure the accuracy of all the Apollo command module engineering drawings. This was inclusive of engineering orders, if not incorporated into the drawings.

Over the course of my first year, I became acquainted with an African American manager named Charlie, who was over a staff of technical specification writers. He was the only manager of color that I knew about, and I eventually became acquainted with only two other men of color in professional positions. I approached Charlie regarding his department's open position for a technical specification writer. He gave me a resume of an individual being considered for the position. I took offense after reading it and said,

"I didn't come here to be impressed by someone's background over my head," and left.

I was wrong!

Charlie still invited me to his home for his Christmas party. He apparently saw potential in me and took me into his kitchen with one of his guests with the intent of providing me with career advice. He said I needed to learn how to "Uncle Tom."

In retrospect, my response was predictable, a bit curt, reflecting a bit of immaturity and wrong regarding my young attitude.

Charlie and the generations before my generation had to learn how to "Uncle Tom" to earn certain management positions. Their acceptance by the senior management made it possible for my generation to achieve higher and greater management/executive positions than the preceding generations. However, I believe the Holy Spirit plan for my career path did not include Charlie's organization.

However, my career path did become tied to a wage and salary analyst, Robert, of whom I met subsequent to my wife's hiring on as a secretary to their manager. The other Tom, I would eventually meet and become a peer to in the Apollo Program Office as a consequence of an open position for which I was recommended. These gentlemen were five years older and my peers and became lifelong friends.

The Apollo Program Office position was one requiring management focus by means of written reports, dispositioning designated Apollo Command Modules, and areas requiring identification of significant problems on critical paths needing management attention and a plan for correction.

Having access to an Apollo Command Module after a Saturn rocket space launch was a tremendous opportunity. We were able to see the effects of air friction in re-entry to earth's atmosphere, burning through the command module's title to its mesh. Seeing the command module's post effects further validated the mandatory title design's needed changes. This experience further broadened my background, and in later years would enhance my resume.

The unexpected social issues and the Watts riot exposed the prejudicial beliefs and attitudes of some of my white/Caucasian peers.

Unfortunately, this racial phobia would be unrelentingly exercised in some management decisions that would eventually impact me and my Black coworker peers. Tom took a position in the Los Angeles Division of North American Aviation, working on the proposal for the U.S. Air Force F-15 Jet Fighter Aircraft. In the latter phase of the Apollo Program, the company became Rockwell International Corporation.

Reflection and Meditating

LIFE'S METAMORPHOSIS OF THE SOUL

CHAPTER 9

New Business and Personal Growth Activation

My peer and friend Tom accepted a position offered on the F-15 Fighter Aircraft Proposal Team at the Los Angeles (LA) Division of North American Aviation. The LA Division also had a proposal team bidding on the B-1B Bomber Program.

After approximately a month of Tom working on the F-15 Fighter Aircraft Proposal, his manager requested he contact me regarding meeting with them for a working weekend luncheon. I was asked to transfer to the LA Division to join with the F-15 Fighter Aircraft Proposal Team. I agreed and the transfer was approved for me to leave the Apollo Program Office.

This working luncheon amounted to a "get to know you and your views/opinions regarding some of the social and civil rights issues on society's current front burners." Our discussions went physiological and set in motion future frank views addressed that pertained to all segments of our culture and society in general.

Tom and I were the only African Americans on the Proposal Team and I became some of the proposal supervision supervisors or team and senior managers' luncheon focal point for much of the front burner issues of the day. I was still attending college in the evening and at times my study time was at University of California at Los Angeles (UCLA) on the weekends. That being the case, I had occasions to hear Professor Angela Davis, Dr. Ron Karenga (the initiator of Kwanzaa: celebration of family, community and culture from Africa) and other intellectuals, having very aggressive debates which influenced how I responded to discussions at times with too much colorful street vernacular.

There was a tremendous learning curve as I worked with the various aspects of meeting and understanding the proposal requirements, both the technical and administrative. Coordinating and working with a sundry of individuals, you begin to understand the differences of temperament, tendencies, personalities, and sensitivities of individuals. This acquired knowledge/experience was most beneficial in dealing with a cadre of individuals.

As a relatively new novice to working on a large proposal such as the F-15 Fighter Aircraft, I was excited about a presupposed win over the aerospace competitor. We had heard a rumor that we would lose the F-15 Fighter Aircraft Program, but the company would win the B-1B Bomber Program. The rumor became a true reality. Consequently, that set in motion a staff reduction. According to company policy, personnel reduction was in general to be based on seniority and experience. As it turned out, some were transferred into the B-1B Bomber Proposal Team but Tom and I, along with some of the other F-15 Fighter Aircraft Team members, were laid off. Tom was given a call the following week, and a couple of the personnel that were laid off shared they had been called and rehired. Apparently, our names came up in discussions. We were told they were warned not to inform us, or they would find themselves out of employment. Unfortunately, racism and prejudicial behavior was still a hard reality. Tom, having a degree was able to get a job within two weeks. I no longer worked in the aerospace industry for nine months out of a 38-year career history.

Reflection and Meditating

CHAPTER 10

Confronting Ego and Pride

Having worked in the aerospace industry nine plus years, this time was a wake-up call to the importance of completing my college education. Even though my experience that was reflected in my resume was impressive, it was submitted to different companies for job positions to no avail. The central point of denial was the lack of a bachelor's degree. The basis of my layoff being racial discrimination and knowing nothing would change the execution of the management decision, it was an incentive for me to always work to a higher standard than my peers.

At this time, I had three very young children. The two boys were grammar school age and a two-year-old girl. I was drawing unemployment insurance, receiving thank you but rejection letters from advertised jobs and working in my father-in-law's hardware store on occasion. Being a 2nd Degree Shotokan Black Belt, I also taught martial arts classes at the YWCA (Young Women's Christian Association) and on occasion taught private lessons. I finally got a job at Toyota Motors working on their shipping and receiving docks.

It's amazing the favor that comes your way when you display an attitude of being grateful for just having a job. The men I worked with daily were always courteous and kind and really mirrored my attitude towards them. How I interacted with them came back to me. My reputation as a good worker made it possible for me to submit my resume to become a mid-level manager. The resume was well received but the lack of a Bachelor of Science degree became once again the offer blocker.

Over the course of the nine months of me not working in the aerospace industry, a true appreciation came for just having a job along with an attitude that reflects one's gratefulness. But just as important, I acquired a greater thankfulness for all a working mother/wife does for her family after working an eight-hour day. Over this nine-month period I realized, through performing, how much many men take for granted when it comes to all that a mother/wife does for a family.

Reflection and Meditating

LIFE'S METAMORPHOSIS OF THE SOUL

CHAPTER 11

Destiny's Calling

There are some preconceived negative experiences we go through as a segue that leads us to the pathway of God's plan into our destiny. After my nine months of being separated from the aerospace industry, I received a call from my past aerospace coworker, Tom, to inform me of a manager at Litton Industry (a developer and manufacturer of the U.S. Navy Aircraft Carrier and Destroyer War Ships) who wanted to interview me. Tom had given him my name.

I truly believe our footsteps are ordered by God. As I pondered this thought, I concluded if Tom and I had not been laid off, or had been called back, our destiny, I believe, would have changed. We both were close to having ten years of employment with the company, which is the beginning qualification for receiving vested rights in the company. This may have been a temptation to remain with the company.

My interview with the Litton Industry manager went well, and I was hired. The position I was offered and received became a true segue into my increasing maturity in business insights and my destiny. Litton Industry had two major contracts with the U.S. Navy to design and manufacture a DD963 Destroyer Ship and a LHA Aircraft Carrier Ship. The position that I was hired for was at the Program Management Office (PMO) level in the support of the DD963 Destroyer Ship. My manager John was a tremendous example of an excellent manager that shared his insights pertaining to how he interacted with key executive managers and his briefing techniques.

Working at the PMO level, I was chosen to work with and support a retired Navy rear admiral who oversaw the engineering design reviews.

For the first time in my aerospace experience, I received a degree of mentorship from my manager John, including organizational insights and the management of personnel. I believe after working a year for John, he saw the potential in me. This belief is based on the time spent with me and what he shared with me that was beyond the aerospace industry. I was also exposed to a location that was in place for executives only. Out of these insights also came some personal relationships and business do's and don'ts. My first business trip to Washington D.C. was with my manager John and other program managers to meet with and brief the Navy customer's leadership and staff.

Occasional social functions initiated by key leadership can invariably lead to personal relationships. John invited me to his social function, which led to the establishment of a personal relationship with a retired Navy admiral named Tim, who was one of the senior managers out of the DD963 PMO. This personal relationship led to areas of common interest, of which one was the building of houseboats. Tim, having lost interest in pursuing the business, gave me all of the various houseboat blueprints and his houseboat builders contacts in Florida.

My father-in-law, being an ambitious man and having sponsored several men from the Caribbean Island of Trinidad & Tobago, wanted to go there to explore the potential for establishing a business.

My father-in-law had a relationship with Trinidad's Commissioner of Oil Inland Revenue, and he arranged meetings with the appropriate government ministries for us.

The building of houseboats was rejected, but there was a great deal of interest for the building of family-related recreational businesses, such as a bowling alley that was chosen as the primary business infrastructure and encouraged by the Government Ministry.

There was a tremendous learning curve over the next four years dealing and negotiating with the various Government Ministries. This venture was a time of confidence building in understanding the modus operandi of the Government Ministries, which demonstrated often unpredictable changes in leadership that led to a lack of timely decision making. I found it most interesting how quickly a joint venture organization found out about our project and the Trinidadian government's interest in the recreational project. The project was like a magnet that drew entrepreneurial interest in the project's potential which eventually led to exploring potential partnerships.

Reflection and Meditating

LIFE'S METAMORPHOSIS OF THE SOUL

CHAPTER 12

The Coming Journey

My working for Litton Industry for two years was a tremendous blessing in unexpected ways as I interacted with not only senior management and engineers of the company, but the various levels of Litton's Navy customers. At the close of a one-on-one meeting with a Navy officer, I was taken by surprise when he asked me if I was going to move to Pascagoula, Mississippi where the ships would be built. It never occurred to me at that time that the ships would not be built in California. My answer was immediate, "No sir!"

Pascagoula had a very nominal aerospace industry business in Mississippi. The location alone was reason enough to decline the offer to move there.

I called and contacted the nearby Hughes Aircraft Company (HAC), Culver City, California, Human Resources Department's Affirmative Action manager. I thought, *"How fortunate and blessed I am because I knew no one, and this manager offered me an immediate interview with himself."*

I drove over to his office, and we spent a substantial amount of time discussing my background. Within an hour of returning to my office, I received a call from the HAC Affirmative Action Manager requesting I return to HAC for a number of interviews. I interviewed with two managers, contractors, Data and Configuration management, and the director of the organization who was also a part of the Program Management Office Organization of which they were all a part of. I received a good offer and gave Litton Industry a two-week notice of resignation.

HAC sold its helicopter business to McDonnell Douglas Aircraft Company and was not a manufacturer of aircraft (commercial, commuter, or military aircraft) of any type. However, HAC was an electronics firm with six operating groups, and all of them engaged aggressively in research and development (R & D) of advanced technology products. The firm was a developer and manufacturer of a multitude of different types of systems and advanced microcircuit technology products for both military and commercial laser and infrared technology, including Asynchronous Satellites, missiles, air and ground base radars, communication systems, etc.

HAC was known for having a history of having very few layoffs and also for having a very large number of active contracts. By my second year of employment with HAC, I had graduated and received a Bachelor of Science Degree. I became the Assistant Department Manager of a staff of 88 (engineers, administrators, computer terminal operators, contractual data administrators, etc.) and a selected key member of the PMO staff of a major Development and Production Program.

As a selected member of the PMO Major Program, you have an active role in all aspects of technical and contractual issues, proposal preparation and negotiations. My position was inclusive of all participating in reviewing and inputting organizations' briefings, reviews, and providing appropriate critiques. The business dynamics set in motion early morning daily meetings with the PMO (many were key members) to work out areas of concern.

During a contractual dispute with the Navy customer, I was tasked to work with the key engineers to identify the proprietary areas on the affected engineering drawings and to coordinate the results with the company's assigned attorneys. Due to the proprietary nature of the engineering drawings, I was allowed to use my manager's director's conference room to complete the task. The director asked me an interesting question that would in later years bring unexpected revelation: "Would you rather be a specialist or a generalist?"

After some discussion, my answer, "a generalist" became obvious based on the different functions within the company I had performed.

Having subsequently briefed the attorney by phone from Culver City of the finalized proprietary completed disposition, I was asked to bring the engineering drawings and meet them in Fullerton at 3:00 p.m. This was on a Friday. My response was, "I am not making that drive that time of day on a Friday."

To my surprise, I received a call within 30 minutes and was requested to be at the helicopter flight line in 30 minutes. I was, for the first time, joyfully privileged to have been flown and waited for, by the company's pilot until our meeting was completed.

There was considerable travel over the following few years to Washington D.C. to be a participant in customer briefings, including contractual negotiations.

Apparently, based on my work history and reputation in the company, I was contacted by Human Resources (HR) requesting I travel with their HR Representative to Berkeley University in Northern California to conduct interviews with some of their graduating seniors for potential job positions within Hughes Aircraft Company (HAC). Subsequently, I was allowed to hire a number of minority interns from Northridge University in Southern California for the summer. At this point in time, I had not known HAC to have previously hired minority interns for the summer. As it turned out, the managers with whom they worked were extremely pleased with their performance. I hadn't realized it at the time, but I was operating once again as an aerospace business generalist.

Reflection and Meditating

CHAPTER 13

Life's Unexpected Divergence

I received an unexpected call from the Vice President of the Electro-Optics Data Systems Group (EDSG) of Technology and Systems Marketing. I knew Harry and he knew me, primarily from past years of my participating in briefing our Navy customer. He had a senior level marketing position open and was given my name by a senior level engineer.

Harry made me an offer, and I reminded him I was also in a managerial position and had the same type of hiring issues he had. I did say to him if he was looking for window dressing, I wasn't interested in the position.

I was made a good offer and accepted it. The expectation I found to be extraordinarily high in that there was no introduction to the engineers I would be expected to work with and no mentoring insights from anyone within the organization. Coming in, I was asked to temporarily work with the department's

Business Operation Office to deal with some financial issues. Going into my third week, I reminded Harry of what I was hired for.

I was initially tasked to support the engineers dealing with reconnaissance surveillance for the gathering of intelligence in areas outside of friendly forces which was considered black and/or a classified world. I was soon contacted thereafter by my boss Harry's counterpart, Chuck, whom I also knew. He notified me that he didn't like my assignment and would not help me. I laughed and told him I didn't ask for help.

He went on to say that my area of assignment was a black world and would probably be too difficult for me to successfully penetrate.

As it turned out, I was tasked to meet a couple of engineers, Trish and Tony, at Dayton Air Force Base in Dayton, Ohio that I would be working with. I flew out over the weekend to meet with them on Monday morning. After meeting with the Air Force customers, we went to the company's field office. It was there I was contacted and directed to go with Trish and Tony to a small company located in Boston,

Massachusetts to meet with two company executives, Elliot and Chuck, to negotiate a small contract.

Subsequent to the negotiations, I spoke with Chuck, my boss' counterpart, and asked for a ride with him and Elliot back to Logan Airport and was politely chastised and instructed to not allow engineers, whom I may be traveling with, to control the transportation and not to take notes when in a negotiation. Elliot, a VP, asked my opinion about the negotiations.

I proceeded to give him my opinion and pointed out what they missed and how they could have concluded the negotiations approximately 30 minutes sooner. Surprisingly, he acknowledged my observation.

Of course, this being my first business venture for the marketing organization, I was exercised by Chuck to go and get their boarding passes while they would go and find the airport seafood kiosk. I went with a great attitude and got their business boarding passes. I was given a first-class boarding pass, without my asking, and a smile. I think I thought at the time, *"Ain't God good!"*

LIFE'S METAMORPHOSIS OF THE SOUL

Reflection and Meditating

CHAPTER 14

A Season of Validation

There were numerous follow-up meetings to the small company with the engineers, Trish and Tony, and myself. This interactive process was not only for ensuring that the contractual areas of concern were understood, but I understood the nature of my job as support to them. After our follow-up meeting with the small company, we met for dinner and Trish expressed her concern that I hadn't taken some notes. She further stated Chuck was wrong for saying not to take notes.

I didn't debate her of her expressed concern of a lack of written notes and agreed to meet for breakfast. I went and wrote an inclusive position paper of our meeting with focus on every aspect of concern, including assigned action items with scheduled completion dates. Trish and Tony were both surprised and acknowledged the position paper was well written.

That one meeting with Trish and Tony, our frank discussions, and my follow-up written position paper took away their concern regarding my capability and writing skills. They stated they would have no problem with my meeting with our customers without them. They acknowledged they were confident that I was an excellent listener and obviously capable of effectively capturing in written form all the necessary areas of focus and concern.

After roughly two years in the marketing organization, it was shared with me there was a strong conjecture in the department that I wouldn't last very long working with the two engineers Trish and Tony. Needless to say, they were all wrong!

My initial assignments and proven performance capability resulted in positioning me to be considered for and/or assigned increasingly more challenging projects, such as an international marketing assignment in Europe, and Artificial Intelligence (AI) & Robotics when the more seasoned marketers did not want it at this early stage of development.

A SEASON OF VALIDATION

I was informed by my boss that one of the senior level marketers was retiring, and no one knew who his points of contacts were or understood his programs status. My boss stated he wanted me to consider taking the position. I didn't comment regarding his expressing wanting me to have the position, but in the meantime, I was given business cards and asked to speak with Jack regarding his programs and contacts.

I had a real concern regarding the potential impact that me taking this position would have on my family. The International Marketer travel schedule was usually two or three weeks at a time. My two sons were grammar school age, and my daughter was in kindergarten.

Suddenly, without explanation, the international offer was off the table. My assumption was that the decision for this sudden withdrawal was to be found at the upper executive level, and the decision was based on the possibility of racial rejection by the European customers. At that point in time, I was okay with the decision.

Soon thereafter, I was given the responsibility to determine the Department of Defense's (DOD) perceived plans for AI and Robotics. I spent a great deal of time researching DOD Program elements that were designated for AI and Robotics to also identify DOD points of contact (POC) which were primarily military, including the company's scientists. Subsequent to all the research and study, I made contacts with those identified as POC for AI to establish a travel schedule to meet with each contact.

In establishing the travel schedule plan, I deliberately set the Hawaiian island of Wahiawa last because I didn't want to give the impression that I was more eager to go there. My instincts said someone in upper management may have that type of belief. However, no one knew I had been there on four past occasions.

Prior to my beginning meetings with my DOD contacts, my initial meetings were with the HAC scientists from the Malibu labs, 1 also, on a couple of occasions, joined with the scientists to attend AI relevant conferences. I acquired a great deal of meaningful knowledge from the early interaction with the scientists.

My subsequent meetings with my DOD military contacts were extremely beneficial based on great interaction and data exchange. In some meetings, I was told by some that I shared with them great insights and they would not forget it. As I was preparing to confirm my last planned meeting in Hawaii, my boss Chuck's boss Eric, decided to cancel my trip without explanation. At the time I thought, *"This is too much an irony, but don't worry about it."*

As I began putting together a final report of the DOD perceived plan directions for AI and Robotics, and overall budgets for AI and Robotics, I coordinated with the HAC Malibu scientist for his thoughts and opinions regarding what I had written. The report went to my boss and upper management. A meeting was set up, and the HAC's six operating groups' key representatives, including the HAC Malibu scientist, were invited to the briefing. The presentation was well received and soon thereafter I was given another assignment.

LIFE'S METAMORPHOSIS OF THE SOUL

Reflection and Meditating

CHAPTER 15

The Unexpected Request

I was accustomed to having to make expected and unexpected adjustments to business decisions and changes. I viewed new assignments as opportunities for growth. This attitude had been with me since I entered the aerospace industry on October 31, 1960. At that time, I knew the importance of my ongoing efforts to continue pursuing my college/university education, but equally as important was my seeking to gain new experience and to expand my knowledge base.

I continued to have a desire to continue embracing every opportunity. Some may have viewed some assignments as one of those undesirable challenges.

However, I chose to see it as a vote of confidence in my proven capability. Consistent accomplishments will invariably translate into one having a noteworthy-great reputation. Your consistent accomplishments will magnify your reputation.

However, it's your consistent behavior that validates the strength of your reputation among your colleagues and customers alike because that reflects the quality of both your character and integrity. A case in point, after spending time in a meeting with my Army customer, I was approached by another customer that knew me. He wanted to discuss another upcoming project that he thought would be of interest to our organization. I subsequently called my boss to share with him the discussion of the incoming Army project just discussed with me by an Army customer. He knew of the project and was surprised at the amount of information shared with me.

My boss Chuck asked to meet with me after I came back from my trip. It wasn't the first time I was the recipient of a customer volunteering to share with me unexpected insights of a program or project for which I had no responsibility, but coincidentally, it was an upcoming program of great interest to my boss.

THE UNEXPECTED REQUEST

My meeting with Chuck took me by complete surprise due to the nature of an unexpected request he made for me to consider. The Hughes Aircraft Company (HAC) had twenty-five Field Business Operation Offices nationally, including Hawaii. There had never been an African American, or any other nationality of color who had managed or worked out of one of these offices. Chuck asked me to think about moving to Michigan. Before I could respond, he asked that I at least think about it.

Admittedly, I had been to Michigan a couple of times and did not care for the state. But on the way home I thought, *"I am about to make a career limiting or enhancing decision."*

Before I even arrived home, I knew I would agree to make the move. I didn't want to hear, *"These Blacks don't want to leave their comfort zone."*

The following week, I was prepared to accept the position offered but was pleasantly surprised to find that one of the senior engineers, a friend, wanted the position. I thought at the time, *"Great! I really didn't want to move from California."*

I didn't think at the time that management had made a decision to move me into another business area to expand my corporate business knowledge.

I left for a business conference that I had to attend in Virginia Beach, Virginia later that week and really gave no further thought to my management's apparent plan for me.

However, upon returning from Virginia Beach, I was informed they wanted me to go to Washington D.C. to meet with the Director of the Air Force that covered programs of corporate interest in the Pentagon. I knew the Director and called to confirm a scheduled meeting time. We met the following week and had a great and encouraging meeting. The final decision was dependent on the V.P.'s approval. We went to dinner while a chauffeur went to the airport to pick up the V.P., who was returning from Europe that evening. Upon the V.P.'s return to the office, he stated he had promised the position to another individual stationed in Eglin, Florida.

I thought to myself, *"That is okay with me because I don't really care to work in Washington*

THE UNEXPECTED REQUEST

D.C," but immediately I was asked to go to Fort Monmouth. I asked, "Where is Fort Monmouth?"

I was told, "New Jersey."

I must admit I was surprised at the high executive level involved in my being moved.

A flight was immediately arranged, and I flew out of Washington D.C. in a rainstorm to Liberty Airport in Newark, New Jersey. Getting up the following morning, I was surprised to find that the rain had turned to snow overnight. My next surprise came when I found the Hughes Aircraft Company (HAC) Field Office and met the manager who was also surprised to meet me. We had just met the previous week at the business conference in Virginia Beach, Virginia. The manager was apparently informed either that morning or the night before of my coming to see whether or not I would be willing to work there, even with the bad, inclement weather that the manager reminded me of. We discussed the position and did agree to my willingness to transfer there and me being hired for the position.

LIFE'S METAMORPHOSIS OF THE SOUL

Reflection and Meditating

CHAPTER 16

The Past and Post Season Beginning

After returning from New Jersey, I met with my boss Chuck to discuss my agreement with the HAC Field Office Manager to transfer into his operation. Chuck did not elaborate on the reason for management's push to get me to transfer to a field assignment. What he did indicate was that this would be a four to five-year assignment and should all go well, I would have an opportunity to have my own Field Office Operation. As I gave thought to my situation, what came to mind was there were 25 Field Office Operations, including Hawaii, the managers of which there had only been male Caucasian managers, but never a minority of any other racial group.

There were absolutely no definite promises for any specific field office but a tentative promise of four or five years to validate my excellent management reputation. I did have in mind the San Diego Field Office, having been there on a couple of occasions in the past when I was doing research on Artificial Intelligence (AI) business potential.

This decision to move from Los Angeles, California was monumental in that our family had never been separated. As it worked out, my youngest son had just joined the Air Force, my oldest son had recently married and was on his own, and my daughter was in high school. My wife and I decided to hire a real estate broker to lease our home out. My wife stayed behind to get our home rented, to move our daughter in with her brother to finish the school year out, and to see if she could transfer from her job in Los Angeles at Continental Airlines to Newark Airport Continental Airlines Customers' Reservations Department.

Unfortunately, the assumed best plan wasn't to be. Even though we hired a professional real estate broker, they rented to husband and wife professional rent dodgers. It took almost two years to get them legally out of our home, leaving considerable damage.

My wife made the move to New Jersey two months after I had moved. Obviously, in such a move comes all of your legal obligations, the expected and the unexpected. My wife had been entrusted over the years to handle our household financial budget and managed to have created substantial unknown debt without my knowledge. As if this wasn't enough, the personal issues of our past that almost destroyed our marriage were still relevant. This revelation of all these issues and problems brought our marriage to an end after 24 years.

Needless to say, my life became increasingly complicated and embarrassing having to inform my boss Chuck of the pending divorce, my having to return all of our furniture at the company's expense, back to Los Angeles and to drive my wife's car across country back to Los Angeles.

Driving across country alone can bring many things back to your memory from many years past that are relevant to your current situation. One particular incident was in going to see my uncle, I saw two doves in the middle of the road, and I thought they would certainly fly off when they heard the car coming. I wasn't driving very fast and they didn't fly off. They literally waited until the car had moved almost from over them when they flew up into the bottom of the car. Needless to say, I felt terrible looking through the rear-view mirror seeing the doves lying dead in the street. I felt it was a prophetic act regarding my marriage that I had never given thought to.

Although the desire on my wife's part was to attempt to reconcile our marriage, I no longer had a desire to do so. I buried myself into understanding all aspects of my new job, inclusive of the customer's position and the organization.

I thought it interesting that Chuck requested, on behalf of a senior R & D engineer I had worked with, for me to return to see the owner of a small R & D technology business whose research was in the area termed edged detection techniques. I felt it was finalizing my latest efforts by writing a position paper on the progress of the technology techniques for the R & D Business Unit.

Reflection and Meditating

_____
_____
_____
_____
_____
_____

CHAPTER 17

The Beginning of the Latter Days of Life

The HAC Fort Monmouth Field Office personnel was comprised of the manager, Edward M., two field office representatives, Vern D. and Pat R., and two administrative secretaries, Diane K. and Jill B.

I sensed that a degree of discontent existed between the manager and the two field office representatives, and it appeared none had ever worked in any of the HAC's six business groups except Pat R. for a short period of time. Pat R. was the previous manager that Edward M. worked for, but the position had reversed upon his return.

My entry into the Field Office Organization caused a change of responsibility which involved a major battlefield network radio program called the Enhanced Position Locating System, being transferred to me along with some R & D projects.

Over the course of the first year, there were consequential interactions and many meetings with my new customer's base to such a degree that some personal relationships became inevitable. My constant coordination was not just with my Fort Monmouth customers, but my company's (HAC) customers confirmed the mandatory necessity for me being the central point to orchestrate the business focus.

Consequently, the HAC customers from the Electronic Devices Group (EDG) meeting with the Fort Monmouth customers resulted in an R & D project award.

Having a solid reputation as a very capable and knowledgeable manager that is highly respected by the Fort Monmouth customer community and the company's group representatives gave access whenever needed. This position not only deals with existing contracts but working to capture new business for designated company groups.

Over the course of the first year, I did travel to California to meet with designated key individuals from the following company's groups with business interest at Fort Monmouth:

Ground Systems Group (GSG), Electro-Optics Data Systems Group (EDSG), and the Missile Systems Group (MSG). I met with them to understand their business interests and to meet the principle Engineers with program/project responsibility.

The manager, Edward M., gave me an excellent performance appraisal, and I was given a promotion to Assistant Manager by the Corporate Vice President without precoordination with the Fort Monmouth manager. Needless to say, it created an uncomfortable situation for me and the manager.

Reflection and Meditating

LIFE'S METAMORPHOSIS OF THE SOUL

CHAPTER 18

The Signs of Change

Just before my second year came, it became evident that changes in the field office would be taking place. Pat R. had returned before the coming year. Vern D. would take a position at Rockwell International, and Craig W. would transfer in from the Missile Systems Group via a corporate decision. While at EDSG on business, I was asked to interview one of their employees, John K., who was being considered for transfer to the Fort Monmouth office. Finally, I was being called at times to address some administrative functions that the manager apparently had failed to complete or do.

The changes experienced were not only in my office organization, but I had become a member of the Industrial Representative Association (IRA), which was an organization of my peers/associates that met on a quarterly basis. I had also become engaged and joined a local church which was very important to my Christian beliefs.

The HAC Corporate agreement with the various airlines made weekend travel a requirement, either going or coming. This agreement was beneficial in that it provided opportunity to see some family and friends. I usually spent some time with my mother and youngest sister TJ and usually attended church with TJ. My sisters and TJ's daughter Tammie are strong Christian believers. My attending church with them exposed me for the first time to tremendous biblical teaching that created a strong desire to study.

Before I became engaged in study, I had a dream at the hotel I was booked in for business in Los Angeles. I dreamt hearing, *"I am the Wheel in the middle of your wheel."*

I immediately thought, *"This has to be in the Bible!"* I soon pursued the search and found the Scripture in Ezekiel 1:15-20. As an immature believer at the time, I didn't understand the significance of having this experience. Locating the Scripture was a conscious awareness of the reality of an action taken by the Holy Spirit.

Having shared this dream experience with my sister TJ, it opened the door for her to call my other sister Claudette and my niece Tammie to see if I wanted to receive salvation. Not that it made a difference, but there was a tremendous downpour of rain that night when I received salvation. What truly surprised me after receiving salvation was the following coming unexpectedly out of my mouth with tears, "I am afraid of failure."

I assume at the time it was because my university degree was in business, not engineering. In later years, I realized that was only partially true because over the course of my career, I had engineers working for me and that would continue to happen on a limited basis throughout my remaining career. The fear of failure was not an obsession, but I grew up not wanting to fail in any thing I wanted to do.

A point of reflection: I was hospitalized on three different occasions with bleeding stomach ulcers because of a troubled marriage. Only my excellent physical condition due to my having become a 2nd degree Shotokan Black Belt Martial Artist, made surgery unnecessary. Unfortunately, I internalized my thoughts and never discussed my painful emotions, nor did I have the maturity to forgive, to trust, or to let go of a revengeful attitude.

In retrospect, my freedom via a peace of mind didn't come until I found myself voluntarily sharing my troubling history with my unknown wife-to-be. For the first time in more than two decades, I was able to let go of all resentment and forgive and trust once again.

Even though my open and frank conversation with my ex-wife was hopeful, it was unilateral, and failure didn't come to mind when I committed to move to Fort Monmouth, New Jersey. In the case of my first marriage failure, it brought a new beginning and a solid contentment of a peace of mind without a reflection of personal failure.

Reflection and Meditating

_____
_____
_____
_____
_____
_____
_____
_____

CHAPTER 19

Promotion and Organization Transition

The increase of HAC Field Office personnel brought a diversity of experienced personnel coming from several of the Corporate Business Groups. That being the case accentuated the lack of effective management experience on the part of the manager, Edward M., who was hired directly out of college and never worked in a corporate business group.

Having never been in the HAC Fort Monmouth Field Office before the previous two years, I was not knowledgeable of the reputation of the manager's management skills. It became evident that the corporate administrative demands for the manager had exceeded his ability to satisfy their demand. I was receiving directions at the time to meet their requests. I was not aware, nor ever told of any corporate issues or concerns regarding the manager's performance. Prior to my promotion to manager of the HAC Fort Monmouth Field Office, there was one retirement, one transfer to the Corporate Office, and one resignation to take a position with an aerospace competitor.

The manager was informed by corporate that he would be officially retired in two weeks. After the decision, he became passively belligerent in his attitude. I had been directed by Corporate to take his office, the company car, and the Field Office bank account. However, I chose to allow him to retain all of the managerial privileges he had, including, before his two weeks' departure day, the closing out of the Field Office bank account that he had responsibility for.

My promotion was officially published throughout the HAC corporation. I was the first African American to become one of the twenty-five Field Office Managers located throughout the contiguous U.S., including Hawaii. One of my first functions was to close down Picatinny Arsenal, the HAC Field Office in Sparta, New Jersey, and take over all of its functions. As a consequence of my promotion, I made travel plans to meet with some of the key executives and engineers with programs, R & D projects and other business interests at Fort Monmouth and other nearby business areas.

This can seem like a coincidence, but I don't see it as such. Upon checking into my hotel room on my first night there, I was awakened to a very literal movement of my covers, beginning at my feet with tucking against my body and methodically moving and tucking against my body all the way up to my head. Admittedly I was afraid to move. As it turned out, this was the same hotel I had stayed at when I had dreamt, *"I am the Wheel in the middle of your wheel"* (Ezekiel 1:15-20). I very strongly felt this was God's Holy Spirit saying to me, "My covering will always be about you."

There is no predetermining time or way when and how the Holy Spirit will deal with you. It can be by way of a dream, a literal physical manifestation of an event or substance, a supernatural experience or encounter, etc. The point is the supernatural experience is just as real as our natural experience.

Reflection and Meditating

LIFE'S METAMORPHOSIS OF THE SOUL

CHAPTER 20

HAC'S Unexpected Leadership Transition

The Howard Hughes Company (HAC) was privately owned by Howard Hughes Medical Foundation. A non-profit corporation forms the inception of HAC and the Hughes Helicopter Corporation which was sold to McDonell Douglas Company Helicopter (Helicopter Company).

After many years of IRS challenges, the Hughes Medical Foundation, a non-profit corporation, HAC agreed it would go public. HAC was sold to General Motors (GM) on December 31, 1985 for $5.2 billion, $2.7 billion cash and 500 million shares of GM Class H Stock. GM merged HAC with Delco Electronics to form Hughes Electronics Corporation, an independent subsidiary.

C. Michael Armstrong, an IBM Executive, became the CEO of the Hughes Electronics Corporation. It was a paradigm shift in leadership in that he was the first non-Ph.D. engineer. He had little background in weapons. He was appointed to head the business and became the Pentagon's largest electronics contractor.

Although Howard Hughes was at times a controversial individual, he as the owner of the HAC had an undeniable impact on the U.S. Military Department of Defense, as well as the commercial airlines industry and the aerospace industry in general. The HAC R & D Technology breakthrough, such as the Asynchronous Satellites, came under the leadership of Pat Hyland, CEO, John Richardson, President, and many experienced engineers that demonstrated excellent leadership and management skills in successfully winning many contracts with advanced technology breakthroughs. I consider myself blessed to have had the opportunity to have known and worked with some of the engineers, senior managers and executives who had a long working history at HAC before its acquisition by General Motors Corporation.

HAC'S UNEXEPECTED LEADERSHIP TRANSITION

Reflection and Meditating

LIFE'S METAMORPHOSIS OF THE SOUL

CHAPTER 21

Moving into a Part of Your Destiny

Legal corporation changes don't necessarily mean there will be instantaneous corporate policy and procedure changes impacting how you execute your function. Most likely your past performance's successful methods will not be altered. Your proven character and integrity having been established, places you in a very favorable position in the eyes and opinions of your management, peers, and associates alike.

Having an excellent work history and reputation with my Army customers, as well as my company's in-house customers, was to some extent based on my working in collaboration with the Army's designated senior engineer and writing technical white papers to bring focus to areas of major concern with suggested recommendations leading to solutions. The effectiveness of generating technical papers led my ex-boss to label me Ernest Hemingway.

LIFE'S METAMORPHOSIS OF THE SOUL

Usually business trips to Fullerton, California, with my Fort Monmouth customers would be for a week. Being required to travel over a weekend invariably allowed me some time to be spent with my family and/or friends. Some degree of time was usually set on the key executive's schedule to be briefed on the current program disposition and to arrange for some one-on-one time between the Army program manager and the company executive.

There are at times unexpected events that have happened on my business trips. I have no explanation as to when such things had begun to happen to me. One day, I was standing in a hotel checkout line when the most bodacious situation occurred to me. Up until this time, out of habit I usually would double check myself to see if my writing pens were in my shirt pocket and whether my wallet was in my suit coat inner pocket, as well as my pocket comb. As I touched my comb, I felt a strong pull on my comb and it literally disappeared. Those standing close by me were probably trying to figure out what I was doing, pulling off my coat and searching through it to find a comb with a broken tooth.

I had never had a physical object on my person to be taken into the spiritual realm. I had no understanding of such an occurrence at this time.

At the time, I only shared this experience with my new wife, Rose, and my sister TJ. I purchased a new comb. This spiritual experience/encounter manifested a degree of an unanticipated level of intrigue. My daily dress apparel for work was suits. Rarely did I wear the same suit under a three-week period of time. The suits I wore had not been taken on my last business trip. Getting home and changing clothes brought forth a shocking surprise at the discovery of two combs in my suit coat's inner pocket – the new one I purchased, and the old one with the broken tooth!

Finally, I believe that the Holy Spirit was making a clear statement that there is more power in the realm of the spirit in demonstrating an inanimate object, the comb, being taken from the natural realm, my suit coat being worn, and then manifesting the comb in another suit I was actually wearing with the new comb and the old comb with the broken tooth in the same pocket of the suit.

LIFE'S METAMORPHOSIS OF THE SOUL

Reflection and Meditating

CHAPTER 22

Come Business and Unrelated Activity

There was at times scheduled business activity requiring travel that surprisingly resulted in a manifestation of a supernatural serendipity experience. On one such occasion, I was able to attend a church with my sister TJ.

I picked her up, and we engaged in our usual conversations of life's generalizations. When we arrived at the church, we parked in the parking lot. I placed my shade eyeglasses in the car console box, and I locked the car.

At the close of the church service, we went back to the car. I opened the car console, and my shade glasses were no longer there. There was security throughout the parking lot, and the car was still locked when we arrived at the car. Even though my sister and I knew I had placed the glasses in the console box, she wanted to go back into the church area where we sat to search for the glasses. It, not surprisingly, was to no avail.

As fate would have it, that same Sunday my sister and I went to breakfast and did not realize our other sister Claudette and her friend Serta had decided to eat at the same restaurant. After breakfast, we went over to my mother's and spent time visiting with one another. I did not know that Serta had the gift of a prophet when she began to speak to me in private. She asked me to come over to the kitchen table where she had a tablet and began to draw a bell-shaped curve. She pointed to the high point on the curve and said, "This is where you are," which was the high point or apex on the curve, and then she pointed to the low point on the curve and said, "This is where you're going, but the Lord will bring you back up."

At the time I had no idea how profoundly accurate her prophecy would be validated until I began to live out the initial part of her prophetic word, years later, regarding a loss of income.

As I gave thought to what I just shared in regards to my at times orchestrating and scheduling business meetings and, at times, travel, it dawned on me that I or others may plan and set and/or schedule meetings, but no one but the Holy Spirit of God can establish when He will allow a supernatural event to take place or a prophetic word to be spoken to you by a chosen vessel of His.

Reflection and Meditating

LIFE'S METAMORPHOSIS OF THE SOUL

CHAPTER 23

A Stirring Up of the Eagle's Nest

There is an appropriate time in which the eagle begins to rustle the nest of its eaglets. Only the parent eagle will determine the exact time of training and releasing its eaglets into the atmosphere and environment that they must be able to exist and survive in.

As an aerospace manager your education, training and experience equips you with the importance of planning, scheduling, and working with others. However, whatever the plans God has determined for your life is only controlled by God, and you don't get a vote. Such as my niece Tammie, who is an anointed prophet and shared the following prophecy, long before the decision was formalized with me, that the U.S Army's Fort Monmouth Army Base in New Jersey would be shut down. It was closed down ten years after my retirement on August 7, 2010 and moved to Aberdeen, Maryland.

In every experience I have had regarding something supernatural, I have experienced a prophetic word or prophecy spoken to me. There is a God reason for that particular time and for each of these events that were in His plan for my life that is tied to His purpose for my life. He alone is the author and the finisher of my faith.

In retrospect, I found it amazing that when I would go to California on business and find time to visit with my sister TJ, she would invariably begin to tell me God has a plan for my life. I usually would not comment, but smile. She would get annoyed with me and tell me to stop smiling and that she was serious.

On one occasion when I was visiting with her, I shared with her my written management analysis that caused my boss to reverse his decision to make a change in my area of responsibility that I didn't agree with. TJ, being the frank sister that she is, said, "Stupid, you don't get it yet. It's the Holy Spirit that gave you the wisdom to write the analysis."

She then shared what she had dreamt about me being in a meeting in the Pentagon and one of the participants was an East Indian that wore a turban. I didn't know what the dream meant, but if the Holy Spirit wants me to know, I know He will open the mind of my understanding whenever it becomes appropriate. I had moved into the season of the Holy Spirit stirring up and rustling my nest. The Holy Spirit is omniscient. He knows all things and would determine and control when these events will be manifesting in my life.

Reflection and Meditating

LIFE'S METAMORPHOSIS OF THE SOUL

CHAPTER 24

Business Expansion and Gateway into the Unforeseen

The Company's acquisition of Magnavox Defense and TI (Texas Instrument) was a substantial increase of the business base requiring an increase in travel. These were businesses located at Fort Monmouth and managed by my peers/associates. I was to take and assimilate these businesses and their managers into my office's business base. The plan was to establish a forward presence of engineers and go after new business.

The task was successfully completed, but the manager of the Field Office Operation had to be approved by the company's CEO. I was confirmed and directed to continue managing the operations. I had to prioritize and expanded the office space to accommodate the forward engineering presence. Two of the added employees forward deployed, were ex-military pilots. I must say all the new employees coming into the field office operations were a pleasure to work with.

Needless to say, travel to the newly acquired companies was necessary but much more to Southern California where the Business Groups and the corporate office were located. Occasional corporate meetings were in Culver City, California, but the majority of those meetings were in Washington, D.C. at the corporate office.

Trips to Southern California on business were like going home and an opportunity to visit with family and/or friends. I would occasionally have lunch or dinner with my wife's lifelong friend, G.T. On one such lunch occasion, I was introduced to an older friend of hers, E.P., who happens to be a psychic. I must admit I knew nothing about psychics. We had a very pleasant lunch, and this older lady began sharing some of her life experiences in her profession. E.P. asked could she see my coffee cup and then asked me what I saw inside of it. I said, "Nothing but coffee."

She then asked could she see my driver's license and asked me to look at it from another angle. I did see what appeared to be an Arab with a beard and turban. This was unchartered water for me!!

E.P. was a very pleasant and likable person who gave me the impression she was a believer, Christian. I would on future trips, when time permitted, have lunch with her. There was a reconnection with G.T. and her future husband, Lo, because of my being able to see them on occasion, when time permitted, from my business meetings. My wife, Rose, and G.T. had been very close and supportive of one another for many years. She called and asked for a financial loan to close on their purchase of a townhouse. We did make the loan, and they did repay it and offered to pay interest which I declined.

Soon thereafter, we were asked to meet with them on the Caribbean Island of Saint Martin for a two-week vacation. We didn't know they had a timeshare and had upgraded it to a penthouse level. We met with them for the next three to four years. Our last year of vacationing with them was after a hurricane ravaged the island. We asked to go to a church that was associated with our church in New Jersey, and Lo declined.

G.T. agreed to go, but I saw a change in attitude and sensed resentment. Obviously, this behavior was totally unexpected, and the relationship came to an unanticipated and unexplained abrupt end.

Reflection and Meditating

CHAPTER 25

Strategy of the Forward Engineering Presence

Establishing an engineering presence in a Field Office Operation was a proactive move to work and get to know their customer counterparts. This allowed frequent collaboration and meetings as determined by the engineers. I attended many of these meetings and gained technical insight into the prevailing challenges.

My technical knowledge base gave me an insight into how I briefed my management, having their business plan in mind, and being more influential in magnifying the importance of improving the connection with customer counterparts at Fort Monmouth. My having access to Fort Monmouth's senior civilian leadership and the Military Command allowed me to be their bridge when needed to accelerate dealing with a concern. This type of action resulted in more frequent communication between senior management executives.

This forward presence of engineers (contractors and customers) collaboratively working together allowed a limited amount of pretesting at Fort Monmouth of the system concepts prior to the much more rigorous field testing in Fullerton before the scheduled program review in California.

My secretary booked me in the Holiday Inn La Mirada in California for the first time. The hotel was nice and convenient to the office. In no way would I be prepared for the beginning transition of a life changing experience. I had showered and shaved, and I went to the closet to get a shirt and tie. I began to put my tie on when suddenly, there was coagulated blood about the diameter size of a half dollar but thicker. It showed a stain on the side of the sink, a stain on the bath towel I stood on, and my shirt had a blood stain on the lower portion. I immediately looked at the bathroom ceiling to no avail. The blood had literally manifested out of the spiritual realm.

I didn't know what to think. So, I took wet Kleenex tissues and began wiping out the blood on the sink which left a difficult stain to remove.

I called my wife and her mother, who had come to live with us, and shared what I had experienced. After work, I spoke with the lady psychic E.P. and asked her what did the manifested blood mean? Her response was, "It beats the Hell out of me, Eddie!"

I never spoke with her again. I only shared the experience with my mother and siblings. No one had an answer, but no one expressed anything about witchcraft. No one that I shared this experience with thought it was something evil, but neither did anyone have an explanation for what it meant. This was another spiritual wake-up call for me that there is a living God! I didn't realize it at the time, but my life in the aerospace industry, including my being moved to New Jersey, had been predestined by God, and in time He would explain the manifested blood. This actual manifestation of blood in my presence was the most powerful turning point in my life. I came to understand that it represented a personal blood covenant that the Holy Spirit established with me. The blood covenant is the most powerful of all covenants. The confirmation of the blood covenant was the coagulated blood that also showed a blood stain on the face of the sink outer portion, a blood stain on the bath towel I stood on and the lower part of my shirt. It is a two-way covenant that declares from God, "All that is in my power, including my life, is yours in your time of need."

One thing I have come to know for certain, the Holy Spirit will intervene in my life when the fullness of His time has come for whatever that situation may be. Even though it was my business focus that brought me to this state of time, He is an omniscient God that had already declared my end from my beginning.

Reflection and Meditating

_____
_____
_____
_____
_____
_____
_____
_____
_____
_____
_____

CHAPTER 26

A Strengthening of My Christian Faith

The strengthening of my Christian faith was absolute in the manifestation of blood in my presence. Even though I was actually in the bathroom looking in the mirror putting my necktie on, the blood was just there as though it was there before I left the bathroom and returned to it. This experience validated the supernatural reality of the realm of the spirit being just as real as the natural realm (but far more powerful) that we see and live in.

We all have a purpose and a gift which God has given each one of us to accomplish the purpose. We also have a destiny and in the fullness of time, I believe God's involvement in your life will be felt directly or indirectly. Regardless of what your profession or situation is, we're not here on earth for no reason. Whatever your situation may be, its accomplishment is important to God, and He chose you to fulfill whatever your purpose and destiny happen to be. Each one of us will invariably have some very difficult challenges that may be part of our life's journey. My grandmother's youngest daughter has three daughters that have had major medical problems all of their lives. The oldest was actually born dead. My grandmother worked with her, and she came back to life. I have never heard my aunt complain about her family situation but she shared my grandmother's direction to her, "Never complain about what God has allowed to come into your life, because He has given you what you need to deal with it."

She passed away at 98 years of age. My grandmother's words of wise counsel have come to me on more than one occasion when I took the time to meditate and reflect on my situation.

Reflection and Meditating

_____
_____
_____
_____
_____
_____
_____

CHAPTER 27

Moving Toward Change

Changes come into your life oftentimes when you least expect. As a businessman in the aerospace industry, especially dealing with any form of engineering systems, changes are commonplace. However, it's a challenge when you receive a directed change such as you must leave the church you're currently attending. My sister TJ said the Holy Spirit said it was time. The pastor had married my wife and me. We had become deacons and had very active involvement in the church.

My wife had been laid off from her job, and we created a non-profit corporation to work with the church. We also worked with the Long Branch School Superintendent to catch those children dropping through the grammar school system's cracks and bring them into the "New Hope" after school program. We convinced the School Superintendent to provide a bus to bring the children to the church and to pay the salaries of teachers that volunteered to work with New Hope. The church finally became a drug-free zone.

My wife Rose was the President of New Hope and was interviewed by the Asbury Park Press in New Jersey because of the success of the program which was one of those lights in a community as defined by President George W. Bush.

In no way did I expect that a business trip to Southern California and a short visit to see my sister TJ would be so she could inform me of the change I must make as directed by the Holy Spirit. It's amazing to know that no matter where you are called, the Holy Spirit will get to you. I must admit this was a difficult thing for me to do because of the close relationships that had developed between us and the pastor. Within a very few weeks of our being informed of what we were to do, the pastor died.

We participated with the church deacons to interact with potential pastors that wanted to be considered to be selected as the replacement pastor. A pastor was finally selected after several different interviews and sermons.

One of my responsibilities as a deacon was to head the audio department. Subsequent to the church service and my selling audiotapes one day, my wife was very upset and said, "We can't go back."

I was joking around and said, "Did someone step on your feet or hurt your feelings?"

She was serious, but I talked her into going back the next Sunday. I still can't explain it as of this writing. That Sunday, I knew when I finished selling the audiotapes that we would not be going back to the church. I called and invited the new pastor to come to my office for a meeting. He did come and I explained to him our leaving the church was a directed spiritual matter we had before the other pastor had died, and it had nothing to do with his becoming the pastor. We went to the church's Thursday evening meeting to address the reason for our leaving the church. We spoke of our love and affection for the church and the congregates in general. But we had to go.

LIFE'S METAMORPHOSIS OF THE SOUL

Reflection and Meditating

CHAPTER 28

International Ministry Transition

I had no idea which Christian church the Holy Spirit was sending us to. My wife had called many churches during the week and failed to communicate with anyone. Even though she left messages, not one returned her calls. We found ourselves on Saturday night not knowing where we would be going to church Sunday morning. Suddenly my wife remembered a coworker inviting her to her church about four years previously. Fortunately, she still had the same phone number and joyfully communicated with my wife for a period of time and gave us directions to Faith Fellowship Ministries in Edison, New Jersey.

Each Sunday morning, we usually watch Christian programs and were quite surprised to see the church pastor, David T. Demola, preaching a sermon. This was the first time out of the past years we had watched this Christian channel that we had seen this church and pastor. When we arrived, we were seated next to a Caucasian lady who spoke to us after the praise and worship service. She said, "The two of you are to be here and will be blessed."

We never saw her again.

We were so pleased with the pastor's teaching and the extraordinarily displayed kindness towards us. We agreed this was the church for us, and we soon thereafter became members. My wife had been out of the workforce for almost four years even though her aerospace experience and university degree had positioned her to be hired by a small company when she moved to New Jersey. Her follow-up interviews with small companies were excellent and promising but never seemed to work out. The interviewer at a small company after reviewing her resume said she would never remain with them even though she took exception. One other small company said she would absolutely be perfect for their position, but the budget was taken away.

After our discussion regarding her interests in attending Rutgers University, Faith Fellowship Ministries started a Christian Clinical

Psychology Degree program with the National Christian Counselors Association (NCCA) based in Sarasota Florida. Rose became one of their first students. In retrospect, I found it amazing how our paths led to more in-depth Christian classes such as Advanced Christian Training (ACT) classes, prayer team members training for members that prayed and explained salvation to new congregates receiving salvation, and two years of the School of Ministry. These were all unplanned decisions with soulish impact.

As you grow and mature in your belief, it will become evident the footsteps of the righteous are ordered by God. As I have written about different experiences in my life, I found that meditating on a particular situation brought clarity to what I am attempting to express.

Reflection and Meditating

___
___
___
___
___
___
___

LIFE'S METAMORPHOSIS OF THE SOUL

CHAPTER 29

An Unexpected Inquiry

I met and spent time with a group VP Leon C. prior to our leaving to Washington D.C. to attend an Army conference. We spent time in which I briefed him on his business interest at Fort Monmouth. Leon took me by surprise when he told me he would soon be retiring. I asked what he was planning on doing. He said he was going to work at the Synagogue he attended. He then asked me had I given any thought to retiring. I said no, and he began speaking of the probable value of my investments as he also counseled me on taking all of my vacation time when it becomes due.

Without realizing it, I had stepped into a time vortex when I found myself thinking for the first time, *"I think I am getting tired of this business because it's all about war."*

As I strolled through the areas with military displays, I was amazed at my thoughts. I ran into an old engineering friend Kaye S. from

Hughes Aircraft Company, who was an influence in my promotion that ultimately resulted in my being sent to New Jersey. He told me he had retired and wanted to know if I would be interested in working for or consulting to an Israeli Company called Messersmith Company. I said, "Not at this time."

I found it to be intriguing this inquiry of my considering retirement and/or consulting for another company would come to me.

Leon C. soon thereafter did retire and began donating his time with the synagogue he attended. Unfortunately, within a few weeks of his retirement, he had a heart attack and died. This was a real wake-up call for me in how precious life is and how we don't know the length of time we have remaining in our lives.

The company had bought a small watch manufacturing facility in Forest, Mississippi, to convert to manufacture its Advanced Radio Network System. We had several meetings there in the past and we had scheduled another meeting there to address some of the discovered challenges. I had coordinated with the appropriate engineers and manufacturing personnel to attend. On the first day of the meeting, I received a call from the secretary of the two-star general who wanted to be at this meeting. I and the Program's Colonel were directed to cancel the meeting because he had been called to the Pentagon.

My secretary arranged for a return flight back to New Jersey. There was only a couple on the flight when I boarded, and a young man boarded and sat next to me by the window. I was working when he took his seat next to the window. Soon he asked what I did. I gave him a summarized explanation, and as we continued talking, the Holy Spirit began sharing things through me that brought tears to the young man's eyes. I think the couple sitting across the aisle, back a row didn't know what to think. We talked all the way to Saint Louis where we changed aircrafts.

After I changed aircrafts and had time to think about what I had just shared with that young man, I was amazed at what the Holy Spirit had done. He called off the meeting with a two-star general because He wanted to give this young man His word concerning the situation he was concerned about. I was blessed because He used me to deliver His message.

Reflection and Meditating

CHAPTER 30

Prayer Is My Direction Finder

In our lives, there are occasional unplanned situations that occur beyond our control. One such incident took place when I went for my annual checkup with my optometrist. He found, without any prior warning, my retina was detached at 10 to the hour as opposed to the typical normal detachment of 15 past the hour. I was rushed to emergency surgery with a retina surgeon. I had very limited sight for a couple of weeks because they applied a gas technique to heal my retina. It healed but left a large scar.

My wife worked at the church at this time and would prepare a lunch for me before going to the church. I had the Christian Bible on CDs and would manage to listen each day to several of them. My sister TJ would call often to check up on my healing process, and I would cite the Shunammite woman's position which was, "All is well" as she went after the Prophet Elisha (2 Kings 4) to heal her son.

Even though her son had died, she would only state when asked about her son, "All is well."

I chose that as my position as well, and I was determining not to contradict God's healing Scripture in my prayers and faith. As it turns out, even though my right eye was scarred, my left eye was fully functional and did not impede my reading or travel.

God is the author and finisher of your faith, and only He knows when His time for you has come to change your life. Once again, like the blood experience that shook my soul, He spoke to me strongly, though not audibly. It was November 30, 1997, at approximately 7:30 a.m. as I was driving to my office. The Holy Spirit said, *"Come out from amongst them!"*

I literally said, "Lord what did you say?"

He said, *"I said, come out from amongst them!"*

When I arrived at my office, I called my wife Rose and shared what had just happened. Of course, she said, "You had better do what the Lord said!"

We flew out to Los Angeles, California for the Christmas and New Year holiday and had not shared what the Lord had commanded me to do with anyone. We were visiting with my sister Claudette in her kitchen. When her friend came in. She did not speak to anyone and came directly to me and said, "Sonny, didn't the Lord just tell you to come out from amongst them? He said don't stay too long. It will be hard on you."

I was so caught by surprise! I asked, "Who told you?"

Brenda, who is a prophet said, "Sonny, you know the Lord talks to me!"

It was without a doubt a call from the Holy Spirit to *shift* my work and career from the secular world of the aerospace industry to Kingdom heavenly commerce. My time had come for a lifelong commitment to serve my God's heavenly Kingdom commerce.

Reflection and Meditating

_____
_____
_____
_____
_____

LIFE'S METAMORPHOSIS OF THE SOUL

CHAPTER 31

Changes That Come with Time

Truly, I knew the Holy Spirit had given me a command to retire from the aerospace industry and not just my job.

The prophet Brenda was used by the Holy Spirit to further strengthen my confidence in knowing when He deals with me. Even though I had never really focused on retiring, I can honestly say I have never regretted it, because I know the Holy Spirit directed me to do so. God being omniscient and my not even understanding, I knew the time had come for this God-directed change.

I met with my boss, a vice president, and informed him of my decision to retire. He wasn't too happy but respected my decision. I felt blessed because I knew some peers and associates as was my predecessor I had worked for, were forced to retire. I had worked a total of 38 years in the aerospace industry. At this point in time, the Holy Spirit directed me to go back to school through my church's ministry and to volunteer my time through my church, Faith Fellowship Ministries.

I began a year of Advanced Christian Training (ACTS) Classes including volunteering time, a month after my retirement. The ACTS classes were prerequisite to the two years required for the School of Ministry. I began parallel study of National Christian Counselors Association (NCCA) Temporary Analysis Profiles, which are prerequisite to taking Christian counseling courses. In my first year of study, I was asked, along with several other men, to help pull cable and put in speakers throughout the new church being built.

As I reflected on our coming to Faith Fellowship Ministries (FFM), it was because the Holy Spirit directed my sister TJ to tell me it was time to leave the church I had been attending for a number of years. He never said where we were to go. As I mentioned before, my wife finally thought of a former coworker from about four or five years past, who had extended an invitation to attend FFM.

CHANGES THAT COME WITH TIME

It's so amazing when the Holy Spirit moves you into a situation, you have no idea what it is about, nor do you know the people involved. The administrative office was in Sayreville, New Jersey but the old church was still in Edison, New Jersey. At the time when I was just an attending congregant, Dr. Leo Natale, Vice President of FFM and President of FFM Counseling School asked my wife and I to come with him. We went into the choir room where the FFM administrator, the pastor's wife with a security person, a Nigerian family, a recently married young couple, the brother of the young husband and the parents of the young men were. It appeared the young husband was possessed by some type of spirit and seemed to be ready to violently threaten his brother. I immediately began speaking in my heavenly language and went and laid hands on him. He went down to the floor. His countenance changed to a state of calmness immediately. I never had such an experience. I spoke briefly to his brother who said he had read some type of book when this strange manifestation seemed to have possessed him. Nothing was ever said to me subsequent to this situation. It appears only the Holy Spirit knew why He had Dr. Natale come and get me. As I reflect on this highly unusual incident, I realize it was a mere prelude of what was to come on this new journey.

Reflection and Meditating

CHAPTER 32

Moving Forward Without Conditions

Moving into this stage of my journey was most satisfying because the Holy Spirit had directed me to go back to school and to volunteer my time. I was so at peace in my obedience, even though I don't know why God chose this church, FFM, and this time of my life to send me here. For the first time in my life, I knew I was called by the Holy Spirit and all that I had done in the past had positioned me for a time such as this. There were no ulterior motives within me for becoming a member of this church.

This new shift in direction resulted in the discovery of unexpected gifts. One such unanticipated encouragement came from one of my ACTS teachers who had tasked the class to read a particular book and to write a report. I was complemented and told I should be a writer. I had an Elder to share with me about a dream concerning himself and his wife going to the

Netherlands to represent FFM. He was surprised at what I shared with him, and he acknowledged what I said to him was very accurate. That one situation resulted in different people coming to me requesting an interpretation of their dreams. I had never given thought to or desired to do interpretations of dreams.

Obedience to the prompting of the Holy Spirit will begin to reveal some semblance of a plan associated with your life. One such experience came at the church I previously attended prior to FFM. As we were about to leave for the 11:00 a.m. service at the previous church we attended prior to FFM, the Holy Spirit spoke to me, not audibly, *"Come into the other room and sit down. I am going to allow you to see what it's like to not have my hedge about you."*

It felt as though I was standing with a long robe on touching the floor. It felt as though it was instantly lifted and lowered equally as quick. I have never felt such fear in all my life! I literally cried all the way to church and resumed crying all the way home. I was being shown the power of God's mercy by virtue of His hedge being in place for all of humanity. No one in this world could exist without God's mercy! In later years I was led by the Holy Spirit to share this revelation with some individuals.

My volunteering to pull cable throughout the church, including putting in speakers, led me to every nook and cranny in the church. There were at times, an unction to pray.

Reflection and Meditating

LIFE'S METAMORPHOSIS OF THE SOUL

CHAPTER 33

The Unexpected Request

Domenick, the FFM church's head usher, was sent by Dr. Leo Natale to find me. Domenick found me pulling cable and said he told him my wife Rose, whom he knew as a student and volunteer now worked for the church.

When I was taken to Leo's office, he said the Lord told him to go and get me. He did not know who I was and called Domenick.

Leo stated he had been in a meeting with the pastor, his wife, the FFM administrator and the bank mortgage holder who was extremely displeased with the church's management of its construction loan. At the close of the meeting, Pastor told Leo he would have to straighten out their problem, even though he knew nothing about the business nor had any involvement with Pastor's management and decisions of the church's construction. When he went to his office, he fell on his face in prayer and heard the Lord say to go and get Ed Dean.

He asked would I help him, and I agreed to do so. To begin with, I asked for all of the bank's correspondence to the church that had not been responded to and their contract. We soon had a follow-up meeting with the bankers to address their many unanswered requests. I provided them with my resume and briefed them on an itemized action plan that would provide actual financial visibility and establish a budget. They stopped the briefing and told the pastor I was to be hired and given my own office. I was then asked to meet with one of the VP's privately. He told me I was to receive a six-figure salary. I then told him I would accept the position, but it would be on a volunteer basis. I did not give them an explanation, but surely, I was sensitive to the fact that the Holy Spirit had instructed me to volunteer my time.

Over the course of the next three and a half years, Dr. Natale and I met with Pastor's chosen construction superintendent, the primary construction contractor, and all of the sub-contractors. Working with a representative of the

THE UNEXPECTED REQUEST

bank, we met with the primary construction contractor, as well as every subcontractor to reduce their contracted costs. Needless to say, this was a super-sensitive time for all involved parties.

Pastor and his wife, and Dr. Natale and his wife had annually taken the FFM church bus to Fort Myers, Florida to its local church and School of Ministry and Christian Counseling School. I received a call from Dr. Natale stating Pastor wanted me to fly there as soon as possible to help work out some international issues they were having concerning the International Pastors and Ministers Conference (IPMC). As it unfortunately turned out on the morning of 9/11, with a stopover in Atlanta Georgia, I was stuck for four days without my luggage.

The 9/11 experience was a horror to our nation, but also a revealer of a selfish attitude of Pastor when it became impossible for me to get there sooner. I accomplished all that was intended without delay or a negative attitude.

LIFE'S METAMORPHOSIS OF THE SOUL

Reflection and Meditating

CHAPTER 34

Discovering My Spiritual Strengths and Weaknesses

My going to Fort Myers to assist both the pastor and Dr. Natale to work out some unexpected international issues that would have a negative impact on the FFM IPMC Conference became a personal eye opener. It wasn't difficult to work out the issues and to brief Pastor on an implementation plan. My surprise came when Pastor asked me to come with him as he circulated to meet with the various congregants. I discovered this was definitively out of my comfort zone. Doing the task was not a problem but following him around, for me, felt like the role of a grubby. Wrong thought!

I shared my thoughts with Dr. Natale and explained that it came from my younger days of my not wanting to be anyone's servant. Out of my own ignorance, my thoughts were not spiritual but carnal. I must also acknowledge the influence of living in the south, Jackson,

Mississippi, the first 12 years of my life in a resentful Jim Crow environment.

Soon after the FFM IPMC Conference, we were blessed to go with the FFM Missionary Group to Israel. It was absolutely one of the best vacations we have ever had.

Going to Jerusalem was like stepping back into history 2,000 years. I was then unexpectedly blessed when asked to baptize 39 congregants in the Jordan River being that I had become a CMI Pastor.

Without any foreknowledge, the Staff Pastor Brother Joe and the Elder Brother Bud asked to baptize me in the Jordan River of which I gladly consented. Of equal interest, Elder Bud's wife Betty came and shared the following with me: Just before I was baptized, three doves came and perched on a tree limb near us and flew off after I was baptized.

There was one other experience that took me back to my very young boyhood along the muddy Pearl River in Jackson Mississippi.

I had slipped and went there for some reason and on the riverbank itself was a springing up of

UNCOVERING MY SPIRITUAL STRENGTHS AND WEAKNESSES

clear cold sweet water of which I felt a need to and did stoop and drink.

Our Israeli guide had taken us to Gideon Springs and came and asked me to stoop with cupped hands like Gideon and the men he chose that all used cupped hands to drink. I eventually thought of the irony of this experience as I reflected on my boyhood experience.

Reflection and Meditating

_____
_____
_____
_____
_____
_____
_____
_____
_____
_____
_____
_____
_____
_____
_____
_____
_____

LIFE'S METAMORPHOSIS OF THE SOUL

CHAPTER 35

Extended Omnibus Responsibilities

God has made me who I am, and I must do what I have been called to do! He said to go back to school and volunteer your time.

With the completion of the church construction, inclusive of the payoff agreements between the bank and FFM, the primary construction contractor and all of the subcontractors, I thought my job was finished. As it turned out, Dr. Natale's needs ceased to be necessary as I, along with the church attorney Phil C. from the firm of Gibbon & Gibbon went in search of another bank.

I found, to my surprise, political behavior not unlike the secular world. This political behavior would eventually manifest in both a personal and business way. I knew very little about the pastor's ex-administrator of FFM who had a questionable reputation. I received a call from the FFM administrator, Pastor's wife, to let me know he and his wife were personal friends of theirs.

I gave him the benefit of the doubt that his reputation as a good home renovator was valid, and I did hire him. It wasn't too long thereafter that an issue with an untrue accusation made by him regarding the church attorney and the bank we were starting to negotiate with undermined us with the pastor. The irony of this did not change the bank but brought different bank terms (i.e. LIBOR) via a representative from Florida.

As it worked out, the new bank terms were LIBOR based and covered the FFM Church in Sayreville and the Ministries' properties in Fort Myers, Florida.

From my perspective, only the Holy Spirit knew the extent to which my volunteering became comprised after being asked: take responsibility for Men of the Word Organization (16 years), FFM Community Development Center, Financial Officer (20 plus years), Clinical Counseling Teacher for the NCCA Master's Program and many other unforeseen requests that would come e.g. representative of FFM with the church attorney in a legal mediation negotiations and working with a Fort Myers Florida Real Estate Agent to sell the church condos, etc. It came back to me that I was a generalist because I worked with so many different organizations in the aerospace industry. But I believe the Holy Spirit has made me an anointed generalist for that which He has called me to do in the Body of Christ (Faith Fellowship Ministries in particular).

To begin with, let me bring focus to the importance of seeking the Holy Spirit's permission before you do what you're requesting and to bear witness to the power of the anointing on you when you are about to do or say something that would be contrary to the will of the Holy Spirit. When I came to understand we would not be moving back to Los Angeles, California, I sought the Holy Spirit's permission to renovate my basement and He responded with, "Yes and the other two floors as well."

As mentioned above, I did hire the home renovator and when I reviewed his appraisal, I discovered he had quoted all the appliances in two separate areas and made a calculation error in my favor in another area. I brought this to his attention, and he claimed it was an oversight. I then gave him additional work to make up the difference in his added costs and credit where he had erred in my favor. He then said, "I have never known a man like you."

The truth of the matter was his reputation for dishonesty had preceded him. As it turned out, I received profits from my market investments. The amount I received was almost the same amount it cost me to renovate. I said to myself, *"God is good."*

A few weeks later, Pastor saw me alone and said to me, "Don't get me wrong, Ed. I have never known a Black man like you."

I did not comment other than to say, "Okay." As I walked away, I did say, "Lord what did he mean by that comment?"

The Holy Spirit said, *"He is looking at a man I had made free when I placed you in your mother's womb. The world and its encumbrances will never have a hold on you!"*

Finally, the power of the Holy Spirit's anointing put me into total shock! The then Governor Jim McGreevy and his entourage came to FFM because of the CDC's Communities Outreach's impact. Unfortunately, the available Board of Directors was ignored by the FFM CDC executive, and I attributed the oversight to political ignorance. There was an entourage follow-up a few months later and a repeat of the same action. I was furious and went to his office to chasten him. I was about to start chewing him out when I heard myself say, "I apologize. It's my fault for not correcting you the first time!" I went and shared this experience with my close friend Dr. Leo Natale, who said, "That is the Holy Spirit."

Reflection and Meditating

_____
_____
_____
_____
_____
_____
_____
_____
_____
_____
_____

LIFE'S METAMORPHOSIS OF THE SOUL

CHAPTER 36

A Time of Challenges to the Soul

Moving forward beyond my fifth year of retirement brought forth anticipated and unanticipated surprises. It appeared there was a beginning shift in the market, and I began experiencing some signs of financial loss from the market. I never stopped supporting the church nor giving tithes and offerings. I must say I was surprised when Pastor suddenly stopped teaching/preaching and came over to me and began to prophesy to me about great wealth coming but said, "I can't explain where it is coming from." Then he went on teaching/preaching.

As I previously stated, working in so many different areas, my being a generalist, it was no surprise to me when Dr. Natale asked me to teach the NCCA Masters' Program.

We also created a Counseling Internship Program that was patterned after the Medical Intern Program. The Counseling Internship

Program was comprised of students from the Doctorate and Masters' Programs.

My wife had earned her Ph.D. Degree in Christian Clinical Psychology and was the Director of Human Resources (HR), but was also appointed Head of the Counseling Department. We performed client clinical counseling, usually after regular working hours throughout the week. This became a period of accelerated clinical Christian counseling, maturity, and growth. This type of experience was completely unanticipated. A great reputation for achieving great counseling experiences resulted in having to establish a waiting list for counseling.

Even though I was never a FFM employee, I was always treated like an honored volunteer employee but an ordained minister. Once again, an unexpected surprise came from Pastor. It had been quite a few months in the recent past when Pastor had prophesied over me regarding great wealth coming to me and that he could not explain its origin. He once again stopped preaching/teaching and repeated the same prophesy without further clarity.

There is no way to explain when a prophetic word will come to you. But truly when the same word comes to you from a different source that knew nothing about the previously spoken word it shakes your soul. Evangelist Steve Brock, who was a part of Evangelist Benny Hinn's ministry and was a guest minister at FFM's mid-week service, stopped teaching and came to me with almost the same prophesy as Pastor's.

I believe there are specific timelines when the Holy Spirit begins to reveal what He has determined will come to be in your life. Once again, only the Holy Spirit knows why He chose Evangelist Marilyn Hickey whom, after she had preached at FFM, I had taken to the airport. She had begun to board her flight, then suddenly she came back up the jetty and began to prophesy that wealth was coming to me. Needless to say, I was shocked because this was the fourth time this prophetic word about great wealth had been spoken to me. I had not consciously given thought to becoming wealthy, but my stepmother, Alice Ruth, had told me many years ago when I was a young boy that I had said I would become rich.

I had so looked forward to the manifestation of this prophetic word as the years began to go by. I had two separate supernatural dreams, the same dream at different times, of a pallet of a large stack of gold bullion outside a closed warehouse on a clean shipping dock ready to be shipped. Finally, the world-renowned Prophet Moses Vey, who was a guest minister, stopped and embraced my wife and I and said, "God has not forgotten what you have done, what you have given and the house."

I thought, *"Another prophetic word,"* but the Holy Spirit said to me, *"No, these were words of confirmation of my words I spoke through the others."*

Reflection and Meditating

_____
_____
_____
_____
_____
_____
_____
_____

CHAPTER 37

A Trying of Your Faith

The footsteps of the good/righteous man are ordered by the Lord (Psalm 37:23). Some of your life experiences and expectations can bring joy or disappointments that are associated with your faith or a lack of understanding the principles of faith. We at times set a time expectation as to when something should have manifested in our lives. There is a set time for whatever God has established to come into your life, and His will shall be done.

Our God is not a cookie-cutter God. He deals with us in different ways. My wife and I were invited to a young couple's home for the first time to celebrate another young couple's appointment to be church elders. We arrived early and were given a tour of their recently purchased home which was beautiful. I chose to remain at their kitchen counter as the young man took the others on a tour of their home. As I sat there alone, the Holy Spirit said to me, not audibly, "This is what I wanted to do for you, but you have stopped me."

Needless to say, I was shocked and did not have a desire to purchase a large home because I was under the impression we would only be in New Jersey four or five years. I could hardly wait to tell my wife what the Holy Spirit had said to me.

The next morning, I sensed the Holy Spirit urging me to go to a specific area in Middletown, New Jersey that I had always really cared for, but in no way could afford. This area had beautiful homes. They were very large homes sitting above the Navesink River. After driving through the area for a while, I heard the Holy Spirit say, *"Go and get Rose."*

When I arrived home, she was just coming in and all I said was, "Let's take a ride." '

She did not have a clue where we were going. Just before I was to turn on to Navesink River Road, the Holy Spirit spoke very strongly, but not audibly, *"Do you dare to believe?"*

I repeated what He had said to Rose, and said, "Yes, Lord!"

Just as Rose said, "Yes, Lord," she stated the Lord just said, "I don't tease my kids!"

We drove throughout the area for a while, and no homes were for sale.

We went through the area every Sunday after church as a habit. This went on for about a month and a half. While at home, Rose came to me and said, "I think the Lord said to go over to the area."

I said, "I believe the home will be by the golf course."

We had never seen a "For Sale" sign in the area. As we were about to go past the golf course, there was a "For Sale" sign on the lawn of a beautiful home across the street from it.

We stopped and wrote down the realtor and their number. Once we were home, I called to schedule an appointment. I was told they would need to see my financials first. I said, "Thank you," and hung up. I then decided to call back to share my thoughts, such as, "If my wife doesn't like what she sees, I may have shared too much of my personal business."

They then proceeded to ask me about financial investments and a few other questions. I received a call within an hour to confirm an appointment.

Only the Holy Spirit could have gotten us a scheduled appointment that quickly. I don't know what financials they checked but the home was valued at several million dollars, and we were treated extraordinarily well. We were then invited to come back for another visit and told they knew one visit wouldn't be sufficient.

The Holy Spirit was truly involved in this process for me to gain the type of experience I had gained on a personal level. I was accustomed to dealing with millions of dollars in the aerospace industry. As they pressed in to close the deal, my response was, "I have to consult with my financial advisor" (i.e. the Holy Spirit).

My last instruction from the Holy Spirit was, *"You are not to go back to the area until it is time to take possession."*

Reflection and Meditating

_____
_____
_____
_____
_____
_____
_____
_____
_____

CHAPTER 38

When My Income Began to Change

Within the first five years of my retirement, I was well into seven financial digits range, with a $100,000.00 line of credit. These early retirement years were quite profitable, and I was supportive of the church with my tithes and offerings and received no income from the church for any work I performed for the church for a period of approximately ten years. I did begin receiving $300.00 a month for teaching courses associated with the NCCA Christian Cliental Counseling Masters' Program.

The Faith Fellowship Ministry (FFM) Administrator requested that I join the Board of Directors as the Financial Officer for their newly formed non-profit Community Development Center which was to be the Community Outreach Arm of the church. It was in the tenth year of the FFM CDC that the Administrator insisted on paying me $2,000.00 per month. My not receiving income from the church over those years was because the Lord had instructed me to volunteer my time and go back to school. I never received any income associated with the spiritual aspects of the ministry.

Even though I was losing substantial income on a regular basis, I continued providing my tithes and offerings prior to meeting my personal obligations. This became a very trying time and a testing of my faith. I did fall behind, which wasn't good, but I did catch up. James 1:2-8 says to count it all joy when trials and tribulations come your way. It's a testing of your faith. As I was ministering to a friend, I heard instructions to give the check I had just received earlier in the amount of $1,500.00 to the church. I ignored the inner voice but heard it a second time. I told my wife what the Holy Spirit had told me, and we agreed I would obey. The Holy Spirit then said I was being taught to give out of my own need.

Financially, things for me became increasingly worse. The financial market crashed, and we lost our investments. We could no longer in a timely manner cover all of our obligations. I found myself wide awake at 3:00

a.m. unable to sleep. I began to pray until I did not know what else to pray. So, I prayed in my heavenly language until I felt I did not know how to pray any longer. I just started calling out to Jesus repeatedly. Then the Holy Spirit spoke, not audible, and said, *"You came into the realm of the Spirit in fear. You serve a living God, and don't you forget it."*

I got off my knees, went to bed and fell asleep right away.

There is a spiritual song that says, "You can't beat God giving, no matter how you try. The more you give, the more He gives to you."

We tend to think only monetarily but it's so much more than that. I had no idea the degree of difficulties that lay ahead, but God did and had an implementable plan ready to go. My wife and I have no family in New Jersey or the Tri-state area. We were invited to go to breakfast after church services two weeks in a row by a young couple. When they came over after the church services, suddenly there were two other young couples with their children. They all knew each other and wanted to go with us to breakfast also. We were pleasantly surprised that they all wanted to be with us. Our spiritual family grew out of this union. The Holy Spirit said to me and I shared with my wife, *"These are the family of your maturity."*

We had no idea what lay ahead, but we thanked God countless times for our spiritual children, brothers, and sisters for their love, kindness, and generosity that have been beyond measure. It's so amazing how the Holy Spirit chose to communicate with me at times. An usher before service came to me and asked could he share a dream he had about me. I said yes. He then said in his dream I had clinched my fist in anger and my face was a bit contorted. He looked at me for an answer.

I said I need to think about that. I began to think about the previous evening, and it dawned on me I had purchased a lottery ticket that exceeded $500 million. I knew buying the ticket wasn't for me, but I attempted to justify it because of the prophetic word I had received from three different people of God years before. So I was frustrated once again, and the usher was right in what he had dreamt. But here is the kicker. One of my spiritual daughters called me approximately a week later. She had stopped alongside of the New Jersey Parkway in tears, and she said the Lord had told her to call me and tell me my wealth is not coming the way I think.

Reflection and Meditating

LIFE'S METAMORPHOSIS OF THE SOUL

CHAPTER 39

God Watches Over His Word to Perform It

There are times when you can enter into a season of despair when your income is insufficient for meeting financial obligations, planned and/or unplanned. There are different types of circumstances that can be attributed to the stress and anxiety that is associated with your financial lack issues/problems. There are life limits to equipment failures whose repairs or replacements are mandatory. It's an inescapable fact that the 2008 Wall Street financial crash that stripped millions of investors of their retirement income was a major factor in their financial insufficiency.

Another major issue was not different types of equipment requiring financial expenditures but property taxes and/or association fees associated with townhouses and condominiums which resulted in some investors losing their homes.

In a mid-week service, the congregation was in praise and worship when one of my spiritual daughters came over to me and said, "Dad, I was in prayer asking the Holy Spirit to heal me of my pain. The Holy Spirit said to me, 'Stop thinking about yourself and go and tell your father, my son, that I love him, and I am going to take care of him.'"

I was absolutely speechless! I had been living for the first time in many years, check to check, of which some who knew us well may have guessed. No one really knew to what degree we were in a struggle. But I was reminded of a Saturday meeting I had participated in near the church. I was going home and was near a business complex when I thought to myself, *"Lord I need to go back to work!"*

The Holy Spirit responded, not audibly, *"I gave you 38 years in business commerce. You're now in Kingdom commerce."*

During the following mid-week church service, one of my spiritual sons and his wife came over and said they wanted to purchase a washer and dryer for us. We had never mentioned anything about our broken washer and dryer. Another spiritual son, who happens to be a plumber, put in a new hot water tank and would not accept payment. There have been so many unbelievable blessings that our spiritual family has made us apart of, such as trips to the Outer Banks in North Carolina, Martha's Vineyard, et cetera. We received tremendous financial support from one of our spiritual sons and his wife when they found out we were four years behind in our property taxes. We were within days of losing our home to a property-predator company.

These experiences are a reminder of the importance of obedience to our God's calling that will bring you blessings that are exceedingly abundant, more than you can think or imagine. Our embracing each other as a true loving family came through being there for one another when needed and frequent fellowship.

Reflection and Meditating

_____
_____
_____
_____
_____

LIFE'S METAMORPHOSIS OF THE SOUL

CHAPTER 40

Believe and Worship God: Appreciate the Blessings

When you're functioning in the purpose of your calling, there are an infinite number of ways God may deal with you. I have so appreciated when the Holy Spirit has released His blessing through others, oftentimes when least expected. In your walk of obedience to God, there is nothing too difficult for God to do. I believe all things pertaining to those called by God are in accordance with His perfect timing for their manifestation. I offer this quote from the Holy Spirit that was made directly to me regarding His blessing to me, "Appreciate the blessing, but keep hold of the Blesser."

I have been blessed to have received very strong prophetic words spoken to me by both men and women of God that have not yet manifested. Like Abraham, I still believe and trust God and know that a long delay in time does not mean God will not watch over His words to perform them. The prophetic words of great wealth and a particular home the Holy Spirit sent us to, I never asked the Holy Spirit for them initially but desired them once I knew God wanted us to have them (e.g. Solomon asked God for wisdom, and it pleased God. So, He also gave him great wealth as well). I have asked myself, *"Why at my age now?"*

I still don't know yet! But I still believe the Holy Spirit will honor what He has declared for me, including healing the retina of my eyes so that I will have my 20/20 vision returned. I found it really intriguing as I prayed with my wife, out of my mouth came, "I believe by the Holy Spirit, 'you have healed my sin-sick soul and made my body whole.'"

This was a reminder of God's concern for the soul of man and the price His son would pay that the Prophet Isaiah would prophesy. This prophesy would take place several centuries before the birth of the Lord Jesus. Isaiah 53:10-12...yet it pleased the Lord to bruise him; he had put him to grief: when I make his soul an offering for sin, he shall see his son, and prolong his days, and the pleasure of the Lord shall prosper in his hand...when I shall see the travail of his soul, I shall be satisfied...and he poured out his soul unto death...

The true cost for the metamorphosis of the soul is His sacrifice which is a reflection of His character, a character mankind should strive to emulate.

The concern for man's soul can be illustrated in Mark 8:36 "...what profited a man to have gained the whole world and lose his soul?" Your soul will be a reflection of the type of character you are known by. Once again, a display of the virtue of our soul should be a reflection of the character template of the Lord Jesus. Hebrews (Ampc) 13:5-6 "...Let your character or moral disposition be free from the love of money, including greed, avarice, lust and craving for earthly positions, and be satisfied with your present circumstances, for He, God himself said I will in no way fail you, nor leave you without support..."

The question for you today is where are you in this metamorphic state of change?

LIFE'S METAMORPHOSIS OF THE SOUL

Reflection and Meditating

CHAPTER 41

Life's Unexpected Effects and Faith

The years of 2019 and 2020 ushered in a major threat to losing my home because of five years of unpaid property taxes due to the financial collapse of the stock market which drastically impacted my retirement income. Then came the pandemic Covid-19 leading to four months of quarantine. This resulted in unanticipated levels of anxiety and stress in our lives and environment. My Christian faith was my stabilizing force that brought me a semblance of peace in trusting in God's promises.

Romans 8:28 "...and we know that God works all things together for the good of those who love him, who are called according to His purpose."

A prophetic word was given to me to expect great wealth by three different God-called individuals, including confirmation of their word by another prophet a number of years later and my having dreamt twice about a pallet of gold bullion blocks sitting ready on a shipping ramp.

As I documented the past prophetic statements spoken to me, including my own dreams, it dawned on me that approximately eight years prior, my sister Claudette's prophetic friend Serta prophetically spoke my income would be drastically lost but the Lord was going to restore it all. It came to my memory when my stepmother was visiting me in Los Angeles. She suddenly told me that when I was a young child, I told her I was going to be rich. I could only say I didn't remember sharing that belief.

Even though this prophecy has yet to manifest, there has been a constant array of unexpected blessings to come from my sister TJ and my spiritual children which I did not ask for, but I was asked by them what did I need. On each occasion, I was in true need. God is never late, but always on time.

I recently received a stimulus financial payment from the government to pay my current property taxes on time.

Because of the Covid-19 pandemic, I lost my church income from the Community Development Center, but I have the faith to believe once again God will provide all my needs to meet my financial obligations. I rest in my faith in the peace Jesus has given me (John 14:27) and His faithfulness to watch over His Words to perform them.

Psalm 37:25...I have never seen the righteous forsaken nor do his children beg for food.

Numbers 23:19...God is not a man that he should lie, nor a son of man that he should change his mind.

Romans 3:4...Let God be true and every man a liar as it is written.

All that we go through in life, especially the challenges, will bring focus to the type of character and integrity that is integral to your soul and will reveal the degree of the transforming metamorphosis of your soul.

Reflection and Meditating

1st Dream
Pallet of Bullion
Gold Blocks

2nd Dream
Epiphany Bush of
Gold Bullion
Blocks

3rd Dream
Shipping Pallet of
Bullion Blocks of
Gold

Illustrated by Courtney D. Juniel

CHAPTER 42

God Is the Author and the Finisher of My Faith

I am still moving forward in a metamorphosis state and recognizing God has not forgotten me and is faithful to watch over His Word to perform it. His Word shall not return unto Him void but prosper where He has sent it. All that the Holy Spirit has communicated to me shall truly manifest in due season. The Holy Spirit has said to me regarding relative promises, *"Suddenly' things willtake place."*

One day unto the Holy Spirit is like a thousand years and a thousand years is like a day. Is there anything too hard for the Lord?

To make the point I shared earlier when I shared with you that the Holy Spirit manifested coagulated blood on the bathroom marble sink at a hotel I was booked in, blood stains on the bath towel I was standing on and blood on the shirt I had put on, I did seek an explanation of the meaning of this manifestation of the blood. I believe the Holy Spirit was saying it is a personal blood covenant He has made with me. The blood covenant is the most powerful of covenants between individuals and groups of people. It is a commitment to make available the entirety of what one has, including their life, to support the other. This covenant doesn't just represent a one-dimensional tactic.

In Chapter 3, I shared the experience that I had at approximately 15 or 16 years of age with my brother's parakeet, Tommy. I had a history of a fear of all fowls that went back to my early childhood. The parakeet had a fear of all humans and wouldn't allow himself to be handled. I was up late doing homework when suddenly I felt Tommy perch on my shoulder. I was amazed especially since the cage door was still closed, which implied that the parakeet was supernaturally translated. I said to myself, *"I could really like Tommy."*

I opened the cage door, and he jumped in and perched on a small swing. I anxiously went in to see the parakeet the next morning, and he was on the bottom of the cage dead. Needless to say, I was shocked! n 2017, the Holy Spirit supernaturally, once again in the summer, exercised His power over the natural realm and over time. My wife and I were having a morning chat when I heard a very aggressive chirping bird. I asked my wife, "Do you hear that bird?"

She said, "No."

The bird continued aggressively chirping. The Holy Spirit brought the parakeet, Tommy, back to mind and He said, *"An evil spirit used a rooster to bring fear on you as a young child, but I sent the parakeet who feared you as well as you fearing him, to remove fear from the both of you."*

That day sitting there talking to my wife, I was allowed to hear Tommy in the realm of the spirit.

All that the Holy Spirit has declared for my life, including my wife's life, shall become our reality. Time has no meaning pertaining to the promises of God. They're yes and amen.

Truly, I have discovered over the course of my life that all things work together for the greater good of those that love the Lord and are called by His name. There is a change in how you think and what you believe that is influenced by the Holy Spirit. Man's attitude and behavior has been innately prioritized and governed as body, soul, and spirit. This can be viewed as the stage of the cocoon in a larvae stage moving into transition for metamorphosis. With the metamorphosis of the soul, you're striving to become governed and prioritized by the spirit, soul, and lastly the body, in this order, which can be viewed as the metamorphosis to be more Christlike. We who believe serve a living God. He is the author and the finisher of our faith!

Reflection and Meditating

ABOUT THE AUTHOR

Rev. Edward L. Dean, Ph.D. is an esteemed minister, counselor, and financial officer whose career began in the Aerospace Industry. Within his 38 years of service at Raytheon Systems Company (RSC), previously Hughes Aircraft Company, he was afforded opportunities to work in several capacities. Rev. Dean's versatility as a manager and team player were illustrated in his transition from hands-on engineering to managing corporate business aspects of RSC from an engineering, research, and marketing perspective. After a fulfilling career in the Aerospace Industry, he retired in August of 1998.

Rev. Dean obtained a BS degree in Business Administration with a focus in Management and Finance from Los Angeles State University. The dynamics of his hands on programs experience granted him extensive knowledge in CMI (Continue Measurable Improvement) Leadership, Front-End of the Business Management and Planning System, Defense/Aerospace Marketing Management, Integrated Product Development (using IPD teams), and Beyond Borders: Ethics in International Business.

Furthermore, Rev. Dean received his Ph.D. in Philosophy in Clinical Christian Psychology from Cornerstone University in 2008, and the cohesion of his passion and wisdom produced a harvest of ministry opportunities. For instance, Rev. Dean is currently the co-founder of *Road of Sweet Eternity, Inc.*, a nonprofit organization, and *Road of Success Coaching and Counseling, LLC*, a for profit organization. Both entities provide coaching and clinical counseling to individuals from numerous walks of life.

Rev. Dean is currently a volunteer staff minister at Faith Fellowship Ministries World Outreach Center, where he has been a faithful member since 1994. He extends his services to the ministry by way of utilizing his gifts to bless others. Rev. Dean serves on the Faith Fellowship Community Development Corporation (FFCDC) Board of Directors as a Financial Officer, where he provides financial oversight as it pertains to FFCDC Executive Leader for its business operations. In addition, he is the Director of the Solidarity Ministries (i.e. Men of the Word, Victorious Women in Christ, and Singles Ministries), which is a FFMWOC ministry established to meet, encourage & providing a forum to disciple, be a point of contact, and a blessing to the church congregate.

He is married to Rev Rose M. Dean, Ph.D. and between them they have six children, nine grandchildren and three great grandchildren. They enjoy golfing and vacationing in the Caribbean.

ORDER INFORMATION

Books are available at Amazon.com, BN.com
Kindle and Your Local Bookstores (By Request)

Please leave a review for this book on Amazon
and let other readers know how much you
enjoyed reading it.

Thank you!

www.ingramcontent.com/pod-product-compliance
Lightning Source LLC
Chambersburg PA
CBHW070752100426
42742CB00012B/2113